WOULD YOU RATHER...?

by Justin
Heimberg
& David
Gomberg

The

BIG Book

Over **1,500** *Absolutely Absurd Dilemmas* to Ponder

Published by Seven Footer Press
247 West 30th Street, 11th Floor
New York, NY 10001

First Printing, October 2010
10 9 8 7 6 5 4 3 2
© Copyright Justin Heimberg and David Gomberg, 2010
All Rights Reserved

Would You Rather...?® is a registered trademark used under license
from Falls Media LLC, an Imagination company.

Design by Thomas Schirtz
Cover design by Junko Miyakoshi

ISBN 978-1-934734-43-8

www.sevenfooterpress.com

ACKNOWLEDGEMENTS

Big Thanks to the following people for their contributions: Paul Katz, Jonathan Stokes, Steve Harwood, Eric Immerman, and Jason Heimberg. Thanks, as always, to Tom Schirtz for his sleek, lightning-quick design and his always entertaining schadenfreude. Thanks to Robert Kempe and Junko Miyakoshi for their constant hard work. Thanks to David Zuckerman for his watchful eye. And thank you most of all to our lord and savior, Ralph Sampson, for his inspiration and strength.

DISACKNOWLEDGEMENTS

We would like to disacknowledge people who say "you have reached… (then they just say the number you just dialed)", Comcast for their shoddy service and iron-grip monopoly, and that guy who wouldn't give us the eggplant parmesan for no reason.

IV

HOW TO USE THIS BOOK

Sit around with a bunch of friends and read a question out loud. Discuss the advantages and drawbacks of each option before making a choice. Stretch, twist, and otherwise abuse your imagination to think of the multitude of ways the choice could affect you. The question is merely a springboard for your conversation.

Everybody must choose. As the Deity proclaims, YOU MUST CHOOSE! Once everyone has chosen, move on to the next question. It's that simple.

If you receive a question directed at females, and you are a male (or vice-versa), you can do one of several things: a) move on to another question, b) answer the question anyway, or c) freak out.

On occasion, we have provided some "things to consider" when making your decisions, but do not restrict yourself to those subjects when debating. There are no limits with this book. Think big. Imagine big. Laugh big.

♥

TABLE OF CONTENTS

CHAPTER ONE

WHO'D YOU RATHER...?

Across the animal kingdom, choosing an appropriate mate is vital to help ensure the survival of a species. Male humpback whales race in an array of flips and stunts so the female can select the mate with the strongest genes, while peacocks fan their magnificent tail feathers to show peahens who's got the most impressive plumed booty. For human beings, choosing a mate (whether it's for life or for a one night stand) is also a skill that must be honed. While the survival of the species may not be at stake, the survival of your self-respect, dignity, and disease-free genitals might be. With this in mind, we offer you the chance to sharpen your natural selection skills, by serving up these difficult dilemmas concerning possible partners. As always, you must choose. Abstinence is not an option.

Would you rather...

have sex with Heidi Montag
OR
Susan Boyle if you had to then listen to each of them sing for six hours straight?

Would you rather...

have sex with Brad Pitt if he gained 150 pounds
OR
Jeff Foxworthy?

Would you rather...

do the Mac commercial guy and get $5000 worth of PC products
OR
do the PC guy and get $20,000 worth of Mac products?

YOU MUST CHOOSE!

Would you rather...

have sex with Kim Kardashian
OR
Ashley Olsen if they exchanged butts?

Would you rather have phone sex with...

Tracy Morgan **OR** Alex Trebek?

T-Pain **OR** Al Gore?

the banker from *Deal or No Deal* **OR** Oscar the Grouch?

YOU MUST CHOOSE!

Would you rather...

have phone sex with Alicia Keys **OR** Sarah Silverman?

Megan Fox after inhaling helium **OR** Chelsea Handler?

Tyra Banks **OR** JK Rowling?

a telemarketer who is trying to sell you something during the phone sex **OR** someone who subsequently requires you to answer a ten minute survey about your call?

Would you rather...

have a partner who will only give you oral sex if you do the "Vrrroooom! Here comes the airplane!" thing with your penis
OR
a partner who automatically shifts into an uncannily accurate Bill Cosby impression during all sexual activity?

Would you... have sex with Tyne Daly daily
to have sex with Keira Knightley, nightly?

YOU MUST CHOOSE!

IT'S ALL RELATIVE

Would you rather...

for thirty seconds, make out with your mom
OR
with a hot curling iron?

Would you rather...

get a lap dance from your grandma
OR
give a lap dance to your grandma?

Things to consider: physical injury, psychological injury

Would you rather...

lewdly bump and grind with your grandfather to hip hop music
OR
give your uncle twenty neck hickeys?

YOU MUST CHOOSE!

Would you rather...

have sex with Spencer Pratt
OR
George Clooney if they exchanged personalities?

Would you rather...

have sex with a perfect 10 but get herpes
OR
have sex with a 2 and get a $10 coupon to Long John Silvers?

Would you rather...

have sex with Katie Couric
OR
Natalie Portman if she gained 100 pounds?

YOU MUST CHOOSE!

Would you rather...

have sex with a hot garbage man **OR** an unattractive rock star?

a porn star **OR** a pop star?

a hot dispassionate woman **OR** a down and dirty ugly woman with a unibrow and a goiter on her neck the size of a Dixie cup?

an incredibly witty sumo wrestler **OR** a mysterious and troubled busboy?

a barber shop quartet whose members make all sexual sounds and exclamations in harmony **OR** a pack of Ewoks?

YOU MUST CHOOSE!

Would you rather...

have snail mail sex (bawdy letters sent back and forth over a period of months)

OR

have sign language sex?

Things to consider: How would you pleasure yourself while signing?

Would you rather...

have sex with Siamese triplet Jessica Albas (male); Johnny Depps (female)

OR

with just the singular version?

Would you rather...

have sex with a man with a 1-inch penis

OR

a 17-inch penis? Oral sex?

YOU MUST CHOOSE!

Would you rather...

have sex with Rosie O'Donnell

OR

have to push her up a steep hill?

Would you rather...

have sex with Sarah Palin

OR

Tina Fey?

What if you had to talk to them for three hours before and after the sex?

Things to consider: The porn *Nailin' Palin* was made shortly after her vice-presidential bid. What other political porns can you think of that should be made? Examples: *Ridin' Biden*, I🏋‍ *Huckabee, Bush!*

YOU MUST CHOOSE!

BY THE NUMBERS

Would you rather...

take it from Kelly Osbourne wearing a 3" strap-on
OR
from Scarlett Johansson wearing a 10" strap-on?

Would you rather...

get a hand job from a perfect 10 **OR** have sex with a 6?

a foot job from an 8 **OR** have sex with a 5?

a knee job from a 2 **OR** have brunch with a 4?

YOU MUST CHOOSE!

Would you rather...

have sex with a Cyclops Angelina Jolie with the arms of a gorilla and the trunk of an elephant

OR

Joy Behar?

Would you rather...

have sex with Orlando Bloom **OR** Tom Brady?

Daughtry **OR** LeBron James?

Robert Pattinson in character as Edward Cullen **OR** Robert Pattinson, the actor?

YOU MUST CHOOSE!

Would you rather...

give the person on your left a massage and "happy ending"
OR
give the person on your right a thorough prostate exam?

Would you rather...

tongue-kiss the person to your left
OR
get slapped by the person on your right?

YOU MUST CHOOSE!

FUN WITH PUPPETS

Would you rather...

have sex with Big Bird
OR
Cookie Monster?

Things to consider: CM's voracious appetite, contracting a Bird Flu STD

Would you rather...

have sex with The Count
OR
Snuffleupagus?

Things to consider: the Count's OCD, Snuffie produces 18 gallons of ejaculate upon orgasm

YOU MUST CHOOSE!

ROBBIN' THE CRADLE

Would you rather...

have sex with the offspring of Josh Duhamel and Fergie when it grows up **OR** the child of Katie Holmes and Tom Cruise?

the offspring of Gisele and Tom Brady **OR** of Angelina Jolie and Brad Pitt?

the offspring of Seal and Heidi Klum **OR** David and Victoria Beckham?

YOU MUST CHOOSE!

Would you rather...

have sex with an auctioneer who speaks in auctioneer inflection during sex

OR

an aspiring rapper who freestyle rhymes during sex?

Things to consider: Try both.

Would you rather...

have sex with the fourth image when you Google "swarthy"

OR

the third image when you Google "albino"?

Things to consider: Make your choice before Googling, then check and see what you are dealing with.

YOU MUST CHOOSE!

Would you rather...

have sex with Lady Gaga and then have to wear her outfits
for a month

OR

have sex with Dame Judi Dench?

Would you rather...

have sex with the 4 out of 5 dentists that recommend Trident
sugarless gum

OR

the 5th dissenting dentist?
Things to consider: Do you like rebels? Rebels with tooth decay?

YOU MUST CHOOSE!

Would you rather have sex...

on the monkey bars **OR** on a seesaw?

on you parents' bed when they are out **OR** in the room adjacent to your parents' room (separated only by a thin wall) while they are home?

in a plane restroom (mile high club) **OR** in a train restroom (4 foot high club)?

in the pit with all those balls in a Chuck E. Cheese play area **OR** in a convertible while it is going through a carwash?

on a bed of nails in private **OR** on a luxuriously soft bed at Mattress Discounters during a Columbus Day sale?

YOU MUST CHOOSE!

17

Would you rather...

have sex with Bono **OR** Elvis in his prime?

Jason Mraz **OR** Jack Johnson?

Dave Matthews **OR** Rob Thomas?
Things to consider: What if each serenaded you first?

Would you rather...

have sex with Beyoncé **OR** Christina Aguilera?

Madonna now **OR** Britney Spears when she turns 50?

Amy Winehouse sober **OR** Amy Winehouse messed up?

Would you rather...

have sex with a die-hard liberal who's conservative in bed
OR
a die-hard conservative who's liberal in bed? Who'd you rather marry?

YOU MUST CHOOSE!

Would you rather...

bang the office hottie on your boss's desk
OR
your high school crush in the principal's office?

Would you rather...

have sex with Steve Carell **OR** Stephen Colbert?

Derek Jeter **OR** Kobe Bryant?

Joel McHale **OR** Robert Downey, Jr.?

Tom Colicchio **OR** Simon Cowell?

The Manning brothers **OR** the Jonas Brothers?

YOU MUST CHOOSE!

Would you rather...

have sex with Kristin Kreuk **OR** Brooke Burke?

Marisa Miller **OR** Adriana Lima?

Sharon Stone in her prime **OR** Kathy Ireland in her prime?

Minka Kelly **OR** Minka the porn star (world's largest-breasted Asian)?

Pelbin Frolkdarp **OR** Lelsgahn Nasklope? (Go with your instinct.)

YOU MUST CHOOSE!

CHAPTER TWO

BAD BREAKS: WEIRD, WILD, AND WARPED

For reasons beyond your understanding, you are about to be stricken with a terrible curse: a crazy compulsion, a deranged deformity, a perplexing personality disorder, or some other brutal-for-you, entertaining-for-everyone-else affliction. Sometimes, a curse can turn out to be a blessing in disguise. Other times, not so much...

Would you rather...

impulsively shout "Follow that car, and step on it!" every time you get into a vehicle

OR

invariably start all your sentences with "Negro, please!"?

Would you rather...

have orange Jell-O phlegm

OR

have glittered sweat?
Things to consider: possible stripper career

Would you rather...

for the rest of your life, have a two inch splinter of wood inescapably stuck in your head

OR

have the song "Afternoon Delight" inescapably stuck in your head?

YOU MUST CHOOSE!

Would you rather...

compulsively police-frisk everyone you meet until "they're clear"
OR
passionately kiss anyone and everyone whenever you say goodbye?

Would you rather...

only be able to express your feelings by bursting into Broadway-style song and dance
OR
only by using PowerPoint presentations complete with charts and graphs?

Would you rather...

realize you have gum caught in your pubic hair
OR
realize you have pubic hair caught in your gum (after five minutes of chewing)?
Things to consider: This question excerpted from the *Socratic Dialogues*.

YOU MUST CHOOSE!

Would you rather...

hear all music in 8-bit Nintendo DS sound quality
OR
mistakenly push on every "pull" door for two minutes before figuring it out?

Would you rather...

automatically bitch slap anyone you're speaking with who makes a grammatical error
OR
be able to defecate only in birdhouses?

Would you rather...

have a government agent on three-way calling for all of your phone calls
OR
have an attention-seeking Dane Cook on three-way for all your calls?

YOU MUST CHOOSE!

Would you rather...

have a harelip
OR
lip hair?
Things to consider: Lip hair is comprised of a dozen 10-inch-long hairs which cannot be cut.

Would you rather...

have all your text messages broadcast on highway amber alert signs
OR
have all your text messages sent to your parents?

Would you rather...

always have to be talking to stay awake
OR
always have to be moving at least 1 mph?

YOU MUST CHOOSE!

Would you rather...

have surgically implanted bull's horns

OR

surgically implanted bull's balls?

Things to consider: the extra weight

Would you rather...

only be able sleep sharing a bed with a manatee

OR

only be able to shower with the Wayans brothers?

Would you rather...

be stuck in a North Korean prison with Jackie Chan

OR

MacGyver?

YOU MUST CHOOSE!

Would you rather...

be overwhelmingly compelled to chase squirrels and mailmen like a dog

OR

have a tendency to casually crawl onto people's laps to take naps like a cat?

Would you rather...

every time you're in a car, have to hang your head out the window like a dog (including when you are driving)

OR

have to take dumps in a litter box?

YOU MUST CHOOSE!

Would you rather...

be mortally terrified of triangles
OR
of the number 4?
Things to consider: pizza slices, the dreaded isosceles, 4:44.

Would you rather...

only be able to communicate using movie quotes
OR
only be able to speak in Lolcat language?

Would you rather...

have all your dates chaperoned by WWE giant, The Big Show
OR
have to invite a pack of Mormon missionaries to every party
you have?

YOU MUST CHOOSE!

Would you rather...

address all women as "Bee-yotch" for the rest of your life

OR

all men as "My Liege"?

Things to consider: business meetings, family dinners, being a contestant on a game show

Would you rather...

urinate out of your left nostril

OR

defecate only via a bio-prosthetic shoulder-mounted rocket launcher?

Things to consider: using urinals, sneezing, aiming for enemies

YOU MUST CHOOSE!

Would you rather...

have constantly sweaty (to the point of dripping) palms
OR
invariably emit a 10-second fart when hugged?

Would you rather...

have living bowel movements that are in the shape of fecal hamsters
OR
randomly puke up a dozen hermit crabs once a week?

Would you rather...

get a tattoo of an accurate ruler up your arm
OR
a tip percentage chart on the back of your hand?

YOU MUST CHOOSE!

Would you rather...

have all the steps in your house replaced with chutes and ladders
OR
have all your furniture made of adjustable Legos?

Would you rather...

fashion underwear out of crumb-filled potato chip bags
OR
wear socks full of centipedes?

YOU MUST CHOOSE!

Would you rather...

have broccoli hair

OR

croissant skin?

Things to consider: healthy snack hair cut, flaking

Would you rather...

lose your teeth every week like a Tiger Shark

OR

shed your skin once a week like a snake?

Would you rather...

have your skin made out of sticky Wacky Wall Walker material

OR

have your body made out of Nerf material?

Things to consider: constantly collecting dirt and lint, getting really heavy in the swimming pool

YOU MUST CHOOSE!

Would you rather...

have to "log-roll" anytime you are standing still to avoid falling over
OR
perpetually have involuntary movements as if you are swatting gnats out of your face?

Would you rather...

every time you yawn, you are transported back to your living room sofa
OR
every time you crack your knuckles, Ben Stein is transported to Norway?

Would you rather...

compulsively head-butt anything you see that's purple
OR
compulsively make out with anything orange?
Things to consider: eggplant, pumpkins, grapes, carrots, Grimace, Oompa-Loompas

YOU MUST CHOOSE!

Would you rather...

be reincarnated as Paris Hilton's toy poodle
OR
Britney Spears' next baby?

Would you rather...

have a rare Tourette's syndrome that causes you to always flip off police officers
OR
one where you uncontrollably moon nuns?

Would you rather...

always have a dead body in your trunk
OR
always have Don Rickles in your passenger seat?

YOU MUST CHOOSE!

Would you rather...

every time you cry, one person is cured of cancer for every tear
OR
every time you get the hiccups, a random Al Qaeda member is killed for each hiccup?

Would you rather...

have a seven-foot-long tongue
OR
seven-foot-long neck?

Would you rather...

have a helium-filled body
OR
a lead-filled body?

YOU MUST CHOOSE!

Would you rather...

have your two top front teeth never stop growing
OR
your two bottom front teeth never stop growing?
Things to consider: vision problems, walking problems

Would you rather...

compulsively engage mailmen in sumo contests to try to belly them off your doorstep
OR
compulsively challenge all baristas to arm wrestle?

Would you rather...

have an actual beehive hairdo
OR
have actual mutton chop sideburns?

YOU MUST CHOOSE!

Would you rather...

have a solar-powered brain

OR

a battery-powered brain?

Things to consider: Who would have your extra battery?, slowing down as power gets low, cloudy days, where would you live?

Would you rather...

occasionally "lose reception" (like when on a cell phone) in conversation and be unable to hear what people are saying

OR

have a belly button that is a black hole that sucks objects within two inches into nothingness?

Would you rather...

snore the sound of a chainsaw

OR

burp with the force of a bathroom hair dryer?

YOU MUST CHOOSE!

Would you rather...

have to wear a Snuggie in public every day
OR
have to wear an eye patch?
Things to consider: playing sports, business presentations, sleeping on airplanes

Would you rather...

have to drink using only an eye dropper
OR
have to eat using only a thumbtack?

Would you rather...

have to keep a hard-boiled egg in your mouth at all times
OR
have an armadillo chained to your leg at all times?

YOU MUST CHOOSE!

CHAPTER THREE

POWERS

Change isn't always bad. Sometimes the best thing that can happen to you is being forced to find a new job, having to move on from an unhealthy relationship, or being beamed with high-potency gamma rays granting you the very minor power to levitate muffins. As you contemplate the following questions, remember: "With great power, comes great responsibility." And remember also: "With very limited power comes very limited responsibility."

Would you rather...

have the ability to extend yellow lights at traffic signals by 5 seconds

OR

be able to refill your gas tank by playing *Air Supply's Greatest Hits* in its entirety on your car stereo?

Would you rather...

for one day a month be able to save your life and reload like in a computer game

OR

be able to musically "montage" in three minutes vast amounts of learning and/or training that would normally take three months?

Would you rather...

have all your blackheads produce beluga caviar when squeezed

OR

have all your whiteheads turn into pearls over the course of a year?

YOU MUST CHOOSE!

Would you rather...

have psychic visions of available mall parking spots
OR
have the preternatural ability to always choose the fastest checkout line?

Would you rather...

be visited by the "Ghost of Your Sexual Experiences Past"
OR
the "Ghost of Your Sexual Experiences Future"?
Things to consider: What would each show you? What would you learn from it?

Would you rather...

be able to mentally watch any DVD by slipping it into your butt crack
OR
be able to get an Internet connection anywhere as long as you're pinching your nipples?

YOU MUST CHOOSE!

Would you rather...

psychically know all the phone prompts to expediently get you to a live customer service person

OR

have the ability to see through egg cartons at the grocery store and know if any of the eggs inside are broken?

Would you rather...

have astonishing ordering instincts and make perfect menu choices in 3.5 seconds

OR

have amazing luck at finding parking spaces with extra time left on the meter?

Would you rather...

be able to change any lamp into Whoopi Goldberg

OR

vice-versa?

Things to consider: How would you use your powers?

YOU MUST CHOOSE!

Would you rather...

be able to see every human's "expiration date"

OR

not?

Things to consider: Dude, that's deep.

Would you rather...

have the ability to mute another person like a TV

OR

be able to change your voice to a Spanish voice-over?

Things to consider: vacationing in Madrid, nagging moms, petulant kids, petulant day-laborers

Would you rather...

have a vagina that can magically validate any parking pass

OR

that can comfortably hold all the contents of your purse?

(Men: Read as "have a partner with...")

YOU MUST CHOOSE!

Would you rather...

have a penis that comes in handy as a bottle opener
OR
a cigarette lighter?

Would you rather...

have retractable claws
OR
functional gills?
Things to consider: tree climbing, necking

YOU MUST CHOOSE!

Would you rather...

have corkscrew toenails **OR** have potato-peeling fingernails?

have silverware fingernails **OR** lockpick toenails?

a retractable toenail knife **OR** a retractable middle fingernail extender that accomplishes the effect of giving the finger?

Would you rather...

have an avatar that is an eagle-creature **OR** panther-creature?

wolf-creature **OR** spider-creature?

emu-creature **OR** Paula Poundstone-creature?

Would you rather...

have lemon-flavored hangnails
OR
have denim scabs?

YOU MUST CHOOSE!

Powers

45

Would you rather...

have the ability to will food to fall out of vending machines

OR

be born with a calculator on your ankle?

Would you rather...

be able to summon swarms of bugs

OR

be able to kill bugs with mini-lasers shot from your eyes?

Would you rather...

be able to spit with the force of a blow dart gun

OR

teleport the gas of your farts anywhere within a 100-foot radius?

Things to consider: killing birds, killing careers

YOU MUST CHOOSE!

Would you rather...

be able to eat unlimited food without gaining weight
OR
be able to eat free in any restaurant?

Would you rather...

have x-ray peripheral vision
OR
have the ability to hear anything exactly 147 feet away?

Would you rather...

be able to come in fourth in any race any time
OR
be able to perfectly forge anyone's handwriting but only when writing the phrase "I want pudding!"
Things to consider: selling forged President Obama-signed photos (where he evidently wants everyone to know he wants pudding).

YOU MUST CHOOSE!

Would you rather...

have eyes that can make anyone you want fall in love with you
OR
have eyes that can turn your enemies to stone?

Would you rather...

have skin that lathers whenever you get wet
OR
have refrigerated pockets?
Things to consider: swimming, reaching into your pockets on hot days

Would you rather...

have the ability to communicate with poodles **OR** pit bulls?

kittens **OR** elephants?

socks **OR** bagels?

YOU MUST CHOOSE!

Would you rather...

be given life-long "butting in line" privileges
OR
life-long "profanity at any time" privileges?

Would you rather...

have an hour-long chat with your 15-year-old self
OR
with your 60-year-old self?
Things to consider: What would you say? What would you ask?

Would you rather...

be able to cure cases of malaria by holding your hand against the foreheads of the infirmed
OR
be able to telekinetically deliver titty-twisters?

YOU MUST CHOOSE!

Would you rather...

every time you sneeze, a $20 bill is hidden somewhere in your house
OR
every time you poop, a $100 bill is hidden somewhere inside the BM?

Would you rather...

have the ability to shrink down to one inch in height
OR
the ability to grow to 100 feet in height?

Would you rather...

have a tape measurer tongue
OR
be able to blow into your own body to make it a flotation device?

YOU MUST CHOOSE!

Would you rather...

have ear speakers that broadcast whatever music you imagine in your head

OR

have the ability to make anyone speak in a Jamaican accent?

Would you rather...

have the ability to control the movements of ants

OR

be able to communicate with birds to direct them exactly where to poop?

YOU MUST CHOOSE!

Would you rather...

have a pony tail lasso

OR

have elastic testicles which you use like a mace to fight crime?

Would you rather...

have anything you touch turn to gold **OR** to Silly Putty?

silver **OR** Nerf?

cheese **OR** become helium-filled?

Things to consider: touching furniture, pets, family, friends, enemies

YOU MUST CHOOSE!

THE POO-POO/PEE-PEE PAGE

Would you rather...

poop fragrant potpourri bundles
OR
be able to beam your pee from your bladder to the toilet?
Things to consider: never having to hold it, leaving bathrooms smelling great

Would you rather...

have your poop come out in a perfectly-stacked pyramid of spheres (like cannon balls)
OR
be able to poop complex domino set ups?

YOU MUST CHOOSE!

Would you rather...

be able to talk to any animal
OR
be able to change into any animal?

Would you rather...

have the ability to see the future, but only one second ahead
OR
have the ability to fly, but only in the inside of airplanes?

Would you rather...

produce fudge in your belly button
OR
be able to fart the tune of any song?

YOU MUST CHOOSE!

Would you rather...

have the ability to temporarily swap your parents with your friends' parents

OR

have the ability to temporarily swap facial features with your friends?

Would you rather...

be able to stop and rewind your life

OR

have a cheat code that allows you to jump ahead and skip parts of your life?

YOU MUST CHOOSE!

Would you rather...

be able to scan documents into your computer with your tongue
OR
be able to weed-whack your lawn with your foot?

Would you rather...

have eyes that can change color to match your outfit
OR
tan in the pattern of desert camouflage?

Would you rather...

have Lego boogers
OR
Lincoln-Log poops?

YOU MUST CHOOSE!

Would you rather...

have thunder and lightning crack every time you arch your eyebrow
OR
have the ability to magically control anyone's hair?

Would you rather...

urinate rainbow colors
OR
fart the works or Rachmaninoff?

Would you rather...

be told the answer to the 439th most interesting question in the universe by God
OR
get $50,000?

YOU MUST CHOOSE!

Would you rather...

have one solid gold toe
OR
diamond nipples?

Would you rather...

have an iPhone app that gives you the exact location of any missing pet
OR
the location of nearby people named Millard?

Would you rather...

have an entire department of the CIA devoted to providing you
up-to-the-minute information on all of your exes
OR
your boss?

YOU MUST CHOOSE!

Would you rather...

be able to toast bread with your armpits
OR
blend food into smoothies by sticking your pinkie into a glass?

Would you rather...

have the ability to mentally control ferrets **OR** parrots?

bees **OR** sheep?

dice **OR** toupees?

Would you rather...

have foldable Swiss army knife devices for fingernails
OR
have nunchucks for hair?

YOU MUST CHOOSE!

Would you rather...

be the best hopscotcher in the world
OR
the best air guitarist?

Dragons Age: Origins players only:

Would you rather...

have the pure power of Shale the golem
OR
a rune of +15 damage to Darkspawn?

YOU MUST CHOOSE!

CHAPTER FOUR

SEX CHANGE

In an era where Internet Porn is consumed like a daily vitamin, and a Cleveland Steamer is considered second base, you might think it would be harder to make your sex life odder than it already is. Guess again. Your sex life is about to get a whole lot more interesting.

Would you rather...

the strength of your erection directly correlate to the number of service bars on your cell phone

OR

have an erection which, like a compass, always points north?

Things to consider: switching to Verizon, camping in the West Virginia wilderness, "spotty coverage"; (Women: substitute "your partner's erection").

Would you rather...

never be able to use the Internet for porn again

OR

never be able to use the Internet for legitimate purposes again?

(Women: substitute "Celebrity gossip" for "porn")

Would you rather...

orgasm once every five seconds, five minutes, five years

OR

high five?

Things to consider: your job, your marriage, your pick-up basketball games

YOU MUST CHOOSE!

Would you rather...

have all your sexual experiences narrated like a nature documentary by Sir David Attenborough

OR

sarcastically commented on by the robots from *Mystery Science Theater 3000*?

Would you rather...

have nipples that have fused into each other like a fleshy handle

OR

have extra nipples in the palms of your hands?

Things to consider: ease of arousal, stumping palm-readers, shaking hands at business meetings

Would you rather...

live with a permanent erection of 1 inch

OR

19 inches?

Things to consider: sex, potential for injury, tucking into your sock

YOU MUST CHOOSE!

Would you rather your porn name be...

First name = your middle name; Last name = the first street you grew up on

OR

First name = favorite meteorological adjective (Stormy, Misty, Snowy, Dewy); Last name = favorite substance (Diamond, Stone, Wood, etc.)?

Would you rather your porn name be...

First name = state you're from; Last name = surname of the celebrity you most look like

OR

First name = any Nyquil-alleviated symptom (Stuffy, Coughing, Sneezing, Aching, etc); Last name = Last name of closest Jewish friend?

YOU MUST CHOOSE!

Would you rather...

have a maximum time limit of 3 minutes to complete all your sex acts
OR
a minimum time of 3 hours—(if you climax before then, you have to start over)?

Would you rather...

your orgasm face appear on all of your photo IDs
OR
always exhibit a perfect emotionless poker face and speak in a monotone during sex, including orgasm?

Would you rather have to seduce people using only...

origami **OR** shadow puppets?

a kazoo **OR** river dance?

Saved by the Bell trivia **OR** prop comedy?

YOU MUST CHOOSE!

Right before you approach orgasm, would you rather...

have your adorable pet kitten nuzzle up against you
OR
have your grandmother leave an audible message on your answering machine?

Would you rather...

during sex, thrust to the rhythm of opening bars
of "Eye of the Tiger" **OR** to the rhythm of "Desperado"?

"Another One Bites the Dust" **OR** "Iron Man"?

"Ice Ice Baby" **OR** "Twinkle Twinkle Little Star"?

YOU MUST CHOOSE!

Would you rather...

have a bizarre condition where your penis is 12 inches when limp
but only 3 inches when erect

OR

one that is 28 inches limp and 6 inches erect?

Things to consider: tying it around your waist like a sweatshirt; rolling it up like a snail shell

Would you rather...

make a progressively higher-pitched, whistling teakettle sound
as you approach orgasm

OR

feel the kickback force of a shotgun when climaxing?

Would you rather...

have your climax always interrupted by a phone call from your mom

OR

by Kanye West rushing in and saying, "I'ma let you finish..."
and then launching into some inappropriate speech?

YOU MUST CHOOSE!

Would you rather...

be able to have sex with any partner, once
OR
be able to have sex as many times as you want
but with only one partner?

Would you rather...

(Men) be celibate except one day per decade with your choice of
Victoria's Secret supermodel
OR
be married to a nymphomaniac Kirstie Alley?

Would you rather...

(Women) have your choice of movie star for a sexual partner once
per decade
OR
be married to a sexually charged Louie Anderson?

YOU MUST CHOOSE!

Would you rather...

have your genitals located on the small of your back
OR
on your left shoulder?

Would you rather...

permanently have your genitals shifted 3 inches to the left **OR** rotated 45 degrees counter-clockwise?

4 inches to the left **OR** rotated 180 degrees?

3 inches to the left **OR** 3 inches higher up?

YOU MUST CHOOSE!

Which of the following strange venereal diseases would you endure if you had to choose one? Which would you least want?

- Alaskan King Crabs
- Eyeball herpes
- Constantly expanding testicles
- an STD that causes a burning sensation when you urinate
- an STD that makes the sound of a bagpipe when you defecate?
- an STD that makes your genitals ooze pickle juice
- an STD that makes your penis lighter than air
- an STD that makes your penis a tension-coiled spring like an April Fool's peanut brittle novelty snake
- an STD that makes you think you are Federal Reserve Chairman Ben Bernanke during sex

YOU MUST CHOOSE!

Would you rather...

have ragtime music magically play any time you have sex
OR
have '70s porn music start to play every time you say something that could be interpreted as double entendre no matter where you are?
Things to consider: "I just need to 'file this memo'."

Would you rather...

be compelled to dry-hump anyone you encounter wearing a visor
OR
have your crotch and left eye exchange places?
Things to consider: poker games, eye patches, golf courses

Would you rather...

all attractive people were severely allergic to your genitals
OR
all of your sexual partners henceforth develop Post Traumatic Stress Disorder?

YOU MUST CHOOSE!

Would you rather...

have a penis that works as a metal detector
OR
a laser pointer?

Would you rather...

never be able to watch porn again for the rest of your life
OR
only be able to watch porn for the rest of your life?

Would you rather...

have sex always take as long as it takes you to complete
the *TV Guide* crossword puzzle
OR
as long as it takes for you to complete the *New York Times* Tuesday
crossword puzzle?

YOU MUST CHOOSE!

Would you rather...

always utter the names of state capitals while climaxing **OR** Biblical quotes?

Greek gods **OR** really bad sound effects of machine guns, explosions, helicopters, etc.?

"Here comes the trolley!" **OR** the song "Flash Gordon" by Queen?

Would you rather...

have the only sexual foreplay that works for you be eyeball stimulation **OR**
having your partner fake you out by pretending to throw a tennis ball?
Things to consider: optometrist visits, challenge/pleasure of taking your contacts out, "Where'd it go? Where'd that ball go?! Yay!"

Would you rather...

have breast implants filled with M&Ms **OR** peanut M&Ms?

bacon bits **OR** living chinchillas?

an entire world like that on the flower in *Horton Hears a Who* **OR** the spirit of Leif Erikson?

YOU MUST CHOOSE!

Would you rather...

during sexual congress, be unable to get Burl Ives' "Holly Jolly Christmas" out of your head

OR

be unable to shake the image of the Harlem Globetrotters?

Would you rather...

while in the throes of passion, accidentally yell out the name of your ex **OR** yell out the name of your partner's mother?

a friend of the same sex's name **OR** your own name?

the names of the 1989 Milwaukee Bucks **OR** "Gary Gnu"?

Would you rather...

only be attracted to freckled, redheaded Asians

OR

albinos under 5'2" with 1400+ SAT scores and 0-negative blood type?

YOU MUST CHOOSE!

Would you rather...

upon orgasm, ejaculate a cup of honey

OR

a gallon of gasoline?

Things to consider: tea, rising gas prices, bear attacks, your carbon footprint

Would you rather...

have an incredible-looking body that is completely sexually nonfunctional

OR

a hideous-looking body that performs amazingly sexually and experiences terrific sensation?

Would you rather...

have cowbells for nipple piercings

OR

pieces of string with helium balloons on the end?

YOU MUST CHOOSE!

PICK-A-PENIS!

Women: Read as "have a partner with…"

Would you rather...

have a penis that is coated with chloroform **OR** one that requires the use of a bike tire pump to get erect?

a light-saber penis **OR** a heatable branding iron penis with your initials on the head?

a penis with a tiny rhinoceros horn on the tip **OR** a penis that wriggles like a snake whenever you hear music?

YOU MUST CHOOSE!

VEXING VAGINAS!

Men: Read as "have a partner with…"

Would you rather...

have a greeting card microchip implanted in your vagina that plays "Feliz Navidad" every time you spread your legs **OR** one that makes the sound of an air horn at orgasm?

a vagina that shoots a barrage of camera flashes like the paparazzi when it gets aroused **OR** one that attracts the paparazzi when it gets aroused?
Things to consider: obstacles to oral sex, pictures on gossip sites

YOU MUST CHOOSE!

If you had to choose one of the following pubic haircuts, which would you choose?

The Don King

Flock of Seagulls

Corn Rows

Lionel Richie-style Jheri curls

1880s Circus Muscleman Handlebar Mustache

YOU MUST CHOOSE!

Would you rather...

(men) have your testicles and eyeballs exchange places
OR
your nose and penis?
Things to consider: scrotal surgery to create transparent holes, erections, perineum odor

Would you rather...

(women) have your nipples and eyes change places
OR
your vagina and nose?
Things to consider: cutting holes in shirts, moving to Middle East to wear burqas and veils

Note: These questions excerpted from Jean-Paul Sartre's *Being and Nothingness.*

YOU MUST CHOOSE!

Would you rather...

fart maple syrup
OR
nitrous oxide?

Would you rather...

have genitalia made of fine crystal which if shattered cannot
be repaired
OR
warped imperfect "Golem" genitalia made from a clay mold
that a 6-year-old attempted to accurately craft?

YOU MUST CHOOSE!

Would you rather...

have nipples that grow an inch a day for the rest of your life and curl up all crazy like those dudes who never cut their fingernails

OR

have perpetually lactating nipples (PLN's)?

Things to consider: babies suckling through crazy straw-like nipples, work as a barista

Would you rather...

have literal silver dollar nipples

OR

literal pencil eraser nipples?

Would you rather...

have nipples that can be shot as poisonous darts

OR

that work like "pop up's" to help you know when roasts are done in the oven?

YOU MUST CHOOSE!

Sex Change

CHAPTER **5** FIVE

EMBARRASSING EPISODES

Putting the "bare ass" in embarrassing.

Comfortable in your own skin? What if that skin was tattooed with the periodic table or the life-size face of Bob Saget? You're about to find out exactly how confident and open you truly are. Cringe and bear these gut-wrenching dilemmas featuring an embarrassment of riches and a richness of embarrassment.

Would you rather...

pole-dance naked on a freezing pole
OR
pole-dance in a g-string in front of your in-laws?
Things to consider: labia/scrotal adhesion to pole; father-in-law

Would you rather...

have all your sexual thoughts automatically tweeted to your parents
OR
vice-versa?

Would you rather...

your Facebook status automatically update with a tally of your
lifetime masturbation total
OR
with the name of the person you last fantasized about?

YOU MUST CHOOSE!

Would you rather...

strip in front of your grandparents
OR
have them strip in front of you?

Would you rather...

have a sex tape turn up on the web of you and an old girlfriend/boyfriend
OR
a sex tape of you and your current partner?

Would you rather...

your ringtone be a recording of the dirtiest thing you've ever shouted in bed
OR
the rantings from a white power rally?

YOU MUST CHOOSE!

Would you rather...

butt-dial your girlfriend/boyfriend while you're complaining about them
OR
accidentally "sext" your mom?

Would you rather...

get caught picking your nose by a coworker
OR
rip a stinky, thunderous fart in the middle of an otherwise quiet staff meeting?

Would you rather...

during your wedding, have visible skid marks on your dress
OR
mistakenly say "Assmunch" instead of your partner's name during your vows?

YOU MUST CHOOSE!

Would you rather...

accidentally wet the bed when staying at someone else's house
OR
clog the toilet at a dinner party (complete with break-the-water-surface-BMs and flooding)?

Would you rather...

have Ken Burns make a five part documentary on your adolescent masturbation habits to air on PBS
OR
have a complete written transcript of your sexual encounters available for download for $29.99 on npr.com?

Things to consider: Doris Kearns Goodwin weighing on your use of a "slut-sock"; slow dissolves from a still shot of your ecstatic face to a tube of KY Jelly; do people read?

Would you rather...

have to always fill up your car's gas tank with your pants down
OR
have to sing Village People songs out loud
while shopping?

YOU MUST CHOOSE!

Would you rather...

wear a tuxedo to work every day
OR
a UPS uniform?

Would you rather...

accidentally email your dirtiest email you've ever written to your whole address book
OR
have all of your private sing-to-yourself moments magically broadcast on YouTube?

Would you rather...

after a night of drinking, wake up next to your boss **OR** someone who works beneath you?

a close coworker **OR** your best platonic friend of the opposite sex?

a first-cousin **OR** a llama?

YOU MUST CHOOSE!

Would you rather...

purposely step hard on the wedding dress train as a bride walks down the aisle at a wedding

OR

cough an audible "Boring" at a funeral?

Would you rather...

get caught attending a Miley Cyrus concert

OR

a Billy Ray Cyrus concert?

Would you rather...

have your Match.com profile written by your mother **OR** father?

your six-year-old nephew **OR** your grandmother?

your ex **OR** one of those spam email writers?

Things to consider: bitter comments from your ex; "It is with the utmost sincerity that I request you achieve a date with me. I have recently come into some money and need your company and bank routing number..."

YOU MUST CHOOSE!

Would you rather...

have to dance a ballet for two minutes in front of your entire office/class
OR
have to sing three pop songs in front of everybody?

Would you rather...

have your last named changed to "Scroteboat"
OR
"bin Laden?"

YOU MUST CHOOSE!

Would you rather...

find out your boyfriend/girlfriend has been blogging about your sex life
OR
that your parents have been blogging about theirs?

Would you rather...

have your sexual encounters watched and critiqued by a focus group
of 18-35 year old males behind a one-way mirror
OR
by *America's Got Talent* judges?

Would you rather...

no matter what you are buying, have the cashier at the
supermarket ask for a price check on extra small condoms
every time you get groceries
OR
every time you get groceries, have to use a checkout lane
full of six old women, each paying by check?

YOU MUST CHOOSE!

Would you rather...

after a night of very heavy drinking, wake up next to this guy

OR

this guy?

YOU MUST CHOOSE!

Would you rather...

star in a herpes medication commercial as a patient for $50,000
OR
as the doctor for $5,000?

Would you rather...

slap your grandmother forcefully across the face
OR
watch the Internet video "Two Girls, One Cup" with her?

YOU MUST CHOOSE!

Would you rather be caught by your partner masturbating to...

pictures of your ex **OR** pictures of your partner's sibling?

an anime drawing **OR** a picture of a neighbor?

a framed photo of yourself **OR** lascivious pictures of Optimus Prime?

Would you rather...

compete in a spelling bee and win, but have a vicious erection the entire time

OR

go out in the first round to spare yourself further embarrassment?
(Women: Please substitute "erection" with "super-erect nipples.")

YOU MUST CHOOSE!

Would you rather...

the full catalog of your sexual experiences be available for rental on Netflix
OR
the full catalog of your parents' sexual experiences be available?

Would you rather...

be caught by your friends in possession of an illicit snuff film
OR
a David Archuleta CD?

Would you rather...

have your mother have to sign a consent form every time you perform intercourse
OR
have to fully solve the *New York Times* Crossword before doing so?
Things to consider: weekly Monday sex

YOU MUST CHOOSE!

Would you rather...

have your genitalia regularly printed on the backs of milk cartons nationwide

OR

your orgasm become a popular cell phone ring tone?

Would you rather...

have your Facebook status always show your latest sexual intercourse duration

OR

have to post at least one picture a month on your Facebook feed from one of your sexual encounters (does not have to show nudity)?

YOU MUST CHOOSE!

Would you rather...

have one sexual encounter a month reviewed and analyzed by sports commentators on ESPN

OR

have your sex life traded on the New York Stock Exchange and regularly reported on CNBC?

Things to consider: commentators using the chalkboard, slow-motion replays; your stockholders furious that you didn't have enough anal in the 4th quarter.

Would you rather...

have your sexual performance criticized by Simon Cowell once a year on national television

OR

by your girlfriend once a week at a family dinner?

YOU MUST CHOOSE!

Would you rather...

knowingly have sex with a trannie once
OR
unknowingly have sex with a trannie for a year?

Would you rather...

walk in on your parents having sex
OR
walk in on your grandparents having sex?

YOU MUST CHOOSE!

Which embarrassing fetish would you rather have?

most robust sexual arousal experienced by defecating in wallets **OR** by dressing up and being treated as a Chinese peasant rice-farmer?

unwavering need to be called "Leonard" to reach orgasm **OR** be unable to reach orgasm unless you grip He-Man dolls in both hands?

compulsion to dry-hump tortoises **OR** undeniable urge to have intercourse with grocery store gumball machines?
Things to consider: gumball machines are considered to be some of the most germ-infested objects in the world; shell scrapes

Would you rather...

have your sex life be a topic on *Meet the Press*
OR
Chelsea Lately?

YOU MUST CHOOSE!

Would you rather...

get a Dirty Sanchez

OR

not have to undergo any deviant sexual act, but have a new sex act named after you that involves giving an enema of melted cheese to one's partner and then having them rectally squeeze it out on party crackers which you two share while sipping a glass of fine port?

YOU MUST CHOOSE!

CHAPTER SIX

PREDICTION: PAIN

Life isn't always a bowl of cherries. Sometimes it's a bowl of cherry bombs that you have to light and then put into your mouth one by one until all of your teeth have been blown out. Such is the case with this lovingly brutal chapter where your imagination is sure to be stretched along with your eyelids, nipples, scrotums, and insides. At least you get to choose the lesser of two very, very painful evils.

Would you rather...

use an ice pick as a Q-tip
OR
use sandpaper as toilet paper?

Would you rather...

be twisted up like a balloon animal
OR
crushed like a beer can?

Would you rather...

bite into a popsicle with your front teeth 20 times
OR
get a paper cut on your eye?

YOU MUST CHOOSE!

Would you rather...

dip your hands in hot oil for 3 minutes
OR
have a circus strongman grab your ass cheeks and attempt to rip them in half like a phonebook for 30 seconds?

Would you rather...

be pegged nonstop for ten minutes with oranges **OR** eggs?

chimp feces **OR** cantaloupes?

Koosh balls **OR** paper footballs?

Would you rather...

have your face repeatedly paddled for five minutes by ping pong world champions
OR
have somebody do the "got your nose" trick and really rip off your nose?

YOU MUST CHOOSE!

EVERYBODY HAS A PIERCE.

Would you rather...

get 5000 piercings wherever you want
OR
1 piercing in your heart?

Would you rather...

pierce your perineum
OR
your uvula?

Would you rather...

pierce your eyeball
OR
your pancreas?

YOU MUST CHOOSE!

Would you rather...

shit out 100 jacks
OR
a whole winter squash?

Would you rather...

have an adult circumcision
OR
cut off your left pinky?

Would you rather...

have a tadpole crawl up your nose and turn into a frog
OR
a spider lay an egg sac in your ear?

YOU MUST CHOOSE!

Would you rather...

have your thumbs smashed by a hammer

OR

have a 5-inch screw slowly screwed into your navel?

Would you rather...

for 60 seconds, kiss a poisonous jellyfish

OR

your mother?

Would you rather...

have to wear a nose ring that is connected to an earring
with a 2-inch chain

OR

have to wear a lip ring connected to a belly-button ring
with an 8-inch chain?

YOU MUST CHOOSE!

Would you rather...

be chased by a swarm of bees **OR** by one really angry German Shepherd?

40 angry pigeons **OR** 3 angry weathermen?

10,000 evil crickets **OR** one randy Burger King mascot?

Would you rather...

use a poison ivy condom
OR
have a sushi chef pack your urethra with fresh wasabi?

YOU MUST CHOOSE!

Would you rather...

get your finger run over by an ice skater
OR
get your balls run over by a roller-blader?

Would you rather...

be strapped to a table and have a drop of water repeatedly drip on your forehead
OR
be strapped to a table and have your eyes continuously pried open as you watch a one-week marathon of *Dora the Explorer*?

Would you rather...

have a pebble sewn into the bottom of your left foot
OR
have a sesame seed lodged uncomfortably and permanently between your front teeth?

YOU MUST CHOOSE!

Would you rather...

have to eat 25 jalapeño peppers for breakfast
OR
swallow 25 live mosquitoes?

Would you rather...

live with the certainty that at some point in your life you are going to be attacked by lions but not know when
OR
know exactly when it is going to happen?

Would you rather...

pierce a metal rod through your genitals
OR
through your nose (you can't remove it)?

YOU MUST CHOOSE!

Would you rather...

for twenty seconds, dry-hump a giant cheese grater naked
OR
stick your face in a fan with the safety plate off?

Would you rather...

get a horrible sunburn on the inside of your skin
OR
eat a salad of poison ivy?

Things to consider: Chew well so it is digested by the time it hits your digestive tract, inability to use aloe, ass-rash

YOU MUST CHOOSE!

Would you rather...

jump through a sprinkler of sulfuric acid

OR

have to keep a 200 degree gobstopper in your mouth
for 2 minutes?

Would you rather...

be used as a human piñata until something comes out of you

OR

be used as a human puck on a giant air hockey table?

Would you rather...

get body-slammed in the ring by World Wrestling Entertainment star
John Cena

OR

have to dress for a week in the pro wrestler T-shirt, underwear,
kneepads look?

YOU MUST CHOOSE!

Would you rather...

get spear-tackled by Shaq
OR
sit in a room with just him listening to the new rap album
he's been working on?

Would you rather...

be groped by a Edward Scissorhands
OR
make out with Johnny Staplermouth?

YOU MUST CHOOSE!

Would you rather...

for 20 seconds, rest the side of your face on a hot grill
OR
chisel off your thumbnail?

Would you rather...

stick your hand in a fan
OR
your finger in Tom Bergeron?

Would you rather...

pass a marble through your urethra
OR
a Wiffle ball through your ass?

YOU MUST CHOOSE!

Would you rather...

your doctor tell you that you have swine flu **OR** shingles?

Athlete's Crotch **OR** incurable anal leakage?

that your hands are turning into lobster claws **OR** you will gain 10 pounds a year for the rest of your life?

in order to survive, you can only eat hay for the rest of your life **OR** that you have "Eskimo-itis" – the condition in which you slowly but quite irreversibly turn into an Eskimo?

YOU MUST CHOOSE!

Would you rather...

have the septum of your nose torn with a staple remover
OR
your toenails shimmied off with a pocket knife?

Would you rather...

stick 400 thumbtacks in your body wherever you want
OR
stick 25 thumbtacks in your sack and use it for a pin cushion?

Would you rather...

have a lobster snap its claw onto your right nipple
OR
onto your Adam's Apple?

YOU MUST CHOOSE!

Would you... give your left nut for all the tea in China?

Would you rather...
get bombed to death by planes dropping slabs of beef
OR
drown to death in a pit of chocolate Magic Shell?

Would you rather...
get sacked by Warren Sapp
OR
"sacked" by Warren Sapp?

YOU MUST CHOOSE!

Would you rather...

have an inch-long splinter stuck in your tongue
OR
between your toes?

Would you rather...

get in a snowball fight against a major league pitcher
OR
be a tackling dummy for an NFL linebacker?

Would you rather...

French kiss dry ice
OR
your aunt?

YOU MUST CHOOSE!

Would you rather...

have your foot run over by a lawnmower
OR
cut off your lower lip with children's scissors?

Would you rather...

get a clumsy haircut using a weed-whacker
OR
shave with an electric knife?

Would you rather...

get hit by a car and become roadkill
OR
be attacked by a pack of zombie roadkill?

YOU MUST CHOOSE!

Would you rather...

suffer 1,000 mosquito bites **OR** 1,000 paper cuts?

1,000 loogies **OR** 1,000 Dutch Oven farts?

1,000 minutes of didactic Dr. Phil therapy **OR** 1,000 minutes in a closet with Bjorn Borg?

Would you rather...

have all of your hairs pulled out one by one
OR
all of your teeth pulled out one by one?

YOU MUST CHOOSE!

Would you rather...

use a Japanese Steak House table as a tanning bed for two minutes
OR
get "spray-tanned" by a flamethrower for 30 seconds?

Would you rather...

bungee-jump with the cord tied around your tongue
OR
around your genitals?

YOU MUST CHOOSE!

CHAPTER SEVEN

LIVE IN A WORLD WHERE...

The world don't move to the beat of just one drum,
What might be right for you might not be right for some.
— Henry David Thoreau

Time to play Deity. The laws of the nation, of nature, of convention will soon bend at your whimsical will. Of course, the great Godthings of the Universe are not completely ceding their Rule. They are handing you two choices with which you may shape the planet. The final decision, however, is in your hands, which, by the way, you are presently fiendishly rubbing together, drunk with power.

Would you rather live in a world where...

wearing skinny jeans actually made you skinny while you wore them
OR
where skinny jeans were legally banned?

Would you rather live in a world where...

everyone's sexual performance was rated with reviews on Yelp.com
OR
where you are legally required to have sex with someone if they have
collected at least 5,000 signatures through an online petition?

YOU MUST CHOOSE!

Would you rather live in a world where...

toilets quantify and loudly broadcast the volume/stink of your poops
OR
where ATM's announce your weight and account balance?

Would you rather live in a world where...

Sarah Palin is President
OR
Snooki from *Jersey Shore* is Secretary of State?

YOU MUST CHOOSE!

Would you rather live in a world where...

Mike Tyson is Speaker of the House
OR
where the *Real Housewives of Orange County* comprise
the Supreme Court?

Would you rather live in a world where...

you could get drive-through intercom therapy with your fast food order
OR
where it was customary to get "happy endings" to every haircut?

YOU MUST CHOOSE!

Would you rather live in a world where...

men were expected to be waifish while women were allowed to let themselves go

OR

where men gave birth?

Would you rather live in a world where...

food can be downloaded

OR

where your dreams can?

YOU MUST CHOOSE!

Would you rather live in a world where...

the average penis length is 2 inches
OR
20 inches?

Would you rather live in a world where...

our laws were voted on not by Congress but instead by a public text message voting system á la *American Idol* (kids are allowed to vote)
OR
where amendments were made by posting laws online and opening a forum to everyone?

YOU MUST CHOOSE!

Would you rather live in a world where...

birds pooped hot fudge
OR
where dogs pooped rainbow sherbet?

Would you rather live in a world where...

social stature is derived from mathematical aptitude
OR
from the height of one's hair?

YOU MUST CHOOSE!

Would you rather live in a world where...

reality shows are accurately named, such as "Washed-Up-Celebrity Apprentice" and "Dancing with People Who Have Just Enough Notoriety to Still be Recognized from Their 15 Minutes of Fame"

OR

where women constantly quote chick flicks instead of guys quoting *Fletch* and *Caddyshack*?

Would you rather live in a world where...

teenagers still went to malt shops and sock-hops

OR

where senior citizens do all their shopping at Hot Topic?

YOU MUST CHOOSE!

Would you rather live in a world where...

cities are infested with floating air sharks
OR
where they are full of giant street squids?

Would you rather live in a world where...

the proportion of non-marshmallow-to-marshmallow pieces
in cereal was inverted
OR
where pressing the button multiple times expedited
the elevator's arrival?

YOU MUST CHOOSE!

Would you rather live in a world where...

when you orgasm, you see God
OR
when you orgasm, a delicious ham sandwich appears next to you?

Would you rather live in a world where...

everyone is required to travel via camel
OR
everyone is required to travel via presidential motorcade?
Things to consider: grocery shopping, right of way at a four-way stop sign

YOU MUST CHOOSE!

Would you rather live in a world where...

all business is conducted in Klingon

OR

where nakedness (with penis-gourd casing) was the preferred attire for formal occasions?

Would you rather live in a world...

with cherry-flavored snow

OR

with Old Spice-scented rain?

YOU MUST CHOOSE!

Would you rather live in a world without...

celebrities **OR** corporate welfare?

hurricanes **OR** monogamy?

Sarah Palin **OR** Spencer Pratt?

Would you rather live in a world where...

cell phone use causes baldness
OR
watching game shows is a laxative?

YOU MUST CHOOSE!

Would you rather live in a world where...

general trivia aptitude is a more desirable trait than athleticism
OR
where politicians must disclose their true motivations?

Would you rather live in a world where...

no one except you has a sense of humor
OR
no one except you has a sense of smell?

YOU MUST CHOOSE!

Would you rather live in a world where...

instead of shaking hands, people greet each other with purple nurples
OR
instead of making out, couples rubbed armpits together?
Things to consider: job interviews, the endings of romantic movies

Would you rather live in a world where...

regardless of where you went to sleep, every morning you always wake up naked and spooning a complete stranger
OR
once a month a siren randomly goes off and you are required to give a "rusty trombone" to the person standing nearest to you?

YOU MUST CHOOSE!

Would you rather live in a world where...

men and women had electrical plugs and sockets as genitalia
OR
where people had their genitals located on their palms?

Things to consider: needing an adapter for sex overseas, clapping or shaking hands

Would you rather live in a world where...

where fingernails were made of taffy
OR
where pubic hair was made of cotton candy?

YOU MUST CHOOSE!

Would you rather live in a world where...

it was typical to have full bars in your office like it was in the '50s

OR

where sexual harassment was permitted like it was in the '50s?

YOU MUST CHOOSE!

Would you rather...

support a law legalizing marijuana **OR** prostitution?

legalizing littering **OR** speeding?

legalizing public nudity **OR** groping Foot Locker employees?

Would you rather...

support a law lowering the drinking age to 18 **OR** the age of consent to 16?

raising the drinking age to 35 **OR** the age of consent to 25?

raising the legal smoking age to 21 **OR** capping smoking at age 40?

YOU MUST CHOOSE!

Would you rather live in...

Narnia **OR** Middle Earth?

The Matrix **OR** *Tron*?

Would you rather live in...

the normal world **OR** Oz (as in the *Wizard of...* by day, the HBO show prison by night)?

the daydreams of a 6-year-old **OR** of a 40-year-old?

YOU MUST CHOOSE!

Would you rather live in a world where...

everyone was a vegetarian
OR
everyone was bisexual?

Would you rather live in a world where...

humans had to migrate south in the winter like birds
OR
where humans gave birth to 300 babies at once, like fish, with one or two surviving past the first year?

YOU MUST CHOOSE!

Would you rather live in a world where...

everyone is allowed a maximum of six minutes of Internet access per day
OR
not?

Would you rather live in a world where...

citizens are allowed to try to beat away parking enforcement officers with Wiffle ball bats
OR
where they are allowed to loot the following stores: Just Lamps, Jo-Ann Fabrics, and Big and Tall shops?

YOU MUST CHOOSE!

Would you rather live in a world where...

every day was in the tone of a teen melodrama **OR** a suspense thriller?

a romantic comedy **OR** a porn?

Real World/Road Rules challenge **OR** a horror movie?

Would you rather live in a world where...

bugs are the only viable food source

OR

where the only piece of entertainment was repeats of *Small Wonder* and *Charles in Charge*?

YOU MUST CHOOSE!

Would you rather live in a world where...

Gilbert Gottfried has a complete monopoly on all voiceover work
OR
Heidi Montag delivers all nightly news based on what she is concerned with?

Would you rather live in a world where...

fog has the stench of a nauseating fart cloud
OR
where wind insults you with increasing pace and cruelness as it picks up?

YOU MUST CHOOSE!

Would you rather live in a world where...

houses are made of gingerbread and candy
OR
where motorized Big Wheels are the primary mode of transportation?

Would you rather live in a world where...

humans were the size of ants
OR
where rabbis were the size of oak trees?

YOU MUST CHOOSE!

Would you rather live in...

the mind of Jessica Simpson
OR
Charles Manson?

Would you rather live in a world where...

cops had the speed of the Flash
OR
where homeless people had the power of flight?

YOU MUST CHOOSE!

CHAPTER EIGHT

WORK AND OFFICE

More than half our life is spent on the job. As species, only the ant and the beaver spend more time working. In fact, the duck-billed platypus spends only two minutes a day working (hunting for food) while spending the rest of the day dry-humping coral (look it up). While we can't all make a living dry-humping coral (or can we?), we can imagine ways to liven up our workplace. Cast a vote on the office politics below.

Would you rather...

commute to work on a jetpack
OR
in a rickshaw?

Would you rather...

work in an office with a nap room
OR
a room where you can break objects against the wall when you're angry?

Would you rather...

have the average work day be in the tone of a screwball comedy
OR
in the tone of a kung fu movie?

Things to consider: copier highjinks, water cooler escapades, using a mouse like nunchucks, learning how to spell nunchucks

YOU MUST CHOOSE!

Would you rather...

your office or cubicle had a magnetic force that kept out anyone you didn't like

OR

a portal that went straight to any one place you desired?

Would you rather...

have a magic business card where whatever you write on it becomes your job for a day

OR

never have to work again?
Note: Sell dumb idea to Hollywood.

YOU MUST CHOOSE!

Would you rather...

be a professional pooper scooper **OR** a prison guard?

a video chat sex actor **OR** a rodeo clown?

George Bush's proofreader **OR** John Madden's masseuse?

Would you rather...

possess a special Jedi mind trick where you can avoid doing things at work that you don't want to do

OR

be able to print any image you think of in your mind?

Things to consider: "I am not the account director you are looking for."

YOU MUST CHOOSE!

These are the circumstances. You and your fellow office workers are pitted against each other in a fight to the death. Each gladiator is allowed one office supply to use as a weapon.

Would you rather fight with...

a stapler **OR** a staple remover?

binder clips **OR** rubber bands?

a hole-puncher **OR** label maker?

one of those compressed-air cans you use to clean keyboards **OR** a mug of coffee?

the copier **OR** paper clips?
Things to consider: describe your technique.

YOU MUST CHOOSE!

Would you rather...

work in cubicles stacked vertically like a Japanese driving range
OR
where each cubicle contains a private toilet and stall door?

Would you rather...

work in an office with no chairs **OR** no windows?

no talking **OR** no Internet?

no lunch **OR** no Fatheads of NBA great Ralph Sampson?

YOU MUST CHOOSE!

Would you rather...

have sex with your choice of coworker with no repercussions
OR
punch your choice of coworker with no repercussions?

Would you rather...

have your office chair replaced with a unicycle
OR
a steel pole with a two-inch diameter?

Would you rather...

have the stall doors removed in the bathroom
OR
have to wipe with Post-it notes?

YOU MUST CHOOSE!

Would you rather...

have your morning commute always be a high-speed race with cops
(if you make it to your office parking lot, you don't get a ticket)
OR
have paintball wars every lunch (winner does not have to work
in the afternoon)?

Would you rather...

have your own commuter lane on the highway
OR
have the car of your choice but no commuter lane?

YOU MUST CHOOSE!

Would you rather...

be fired for freezing your company's computer network by surfing for too much porn
OR
for getting drunk at the office holiday party and loudly propositioning your boss?

Would you rather...

outsource all the annoying parts of your job
OR
outsource all the responsibilities of your personal life?

YOU MUST CHOOSE!

Would you rather...

to fulfill a fantasy, receive oral sex while driving
OR
while sitting at your office desk?

Would you rather...

have sex with all the members of your office's IT department
OR
the janitorial staff?

YOU MUST CHOOSE!

Would you rather...

become internationally famous for your booger art
OR
for being an obnoxious reality show star?

Would you rather...

be a gardener with severe allergies **OR** a high school math teacher with problem flatulence?

a blind matador **OR** a quadraplegic luger?

a dyslexic eye doctor **OR** a deaf/mute ventriloquist?

YOU MUST CHOOSE!

Would you rather...

give all business presentations in mime
OR
in the persona and attire of ex-WWE wrestler the Mountie?

Would you rather...

have a calendar in your office of the 12 largest human poops of the past year
OR
the 12 most embarrassing pictures ever taken of you?

Idea for book: *Stinkblots*—like inkblots, but featuring pictures of different fecal creations from which you describe what you images emerge: a butterfly, a caterpillar, your mother, etc.

YOU MUST CHOOSE!

Would you rather...

your boss looked like Megan Fox/George Clooney but acts like a boot camp drill seargant

OR

looked like the Elephant Man but is supportive and encouraging?

Would you rather...

commute to work daily in a Lexus in horrible rush hour traffic

OR

have a quick painless commute but have to drive in a van with a massive Wizard fantasy scene airbrushed on the side?

YOU MUST CHOOSE!

Would you rather...

only be able to communicate with coworkers via email **OR** walkie-talkie?

lifeguard flags **OR** Pictionary?

carrier pigeon **OR** a language consisting of slaps and caresses to the face?

Would you rather...

work at a company where promotions were awarded based on "dance-offs"

OR

battle rapping?

YOU MUST CHOOSE!

Would you rather...

work at a company where mandatory business attire consisted of covering yourself solely in Post-it notes

OR

wearing a sombrero, a Knight Rider half-shirt, a thong, and snowshoes?

Would you rather...

work where they offer a free 4-star-restaurant lunch every day

OR

guilt-free "happy ending" massages every day?

Would you rather...

Oscar Gamble be your boss

OR

your lover?

YOU MUST CHOOSE!

Would you rather...

have to work an 18-hour work day every day
OR
have a 3-hour work day but have to make out with the rest of the employees for 45 minutes each day?

Would you rather...

work as the assistant to (insert least favorite celebrity)
OR
as the personal wiper of (insert favorite celebrity)?

YOU MUST CHOOSE!

Would you rather...

work in Big Tobacco **OR** Big Oil?

Big Pharma **OR** Big Coal?

Big Sock **OR** Big Muffin?

Would you rather...

get paid in pennies
OR
get paid your accrued salary once every three years?

YOU MUST CHOOSE!

CHAPTER NINE

WHO'D YOU RATHER...?
(NON-SEXUAL)

It has been said that the best way to judge a person is by the company he keeps. Batman is no better than Robin. The Scarecrow's worth? Dictated by Mrs. King. Hardcastle: McCormick. Simon? Simon. So choose your friends wisely. And choose your enemies wisely-er.

Would you rather have to solve crimes teamed up with...

Gary Busey **OR** Jessica Simpson?

Betty White **OR** Donald Trump?

your mother **OR** your father?

Would you rather...

be tennis partners with Kim Jong Il
OR
a drunken Mel Gibson?
Things to consider: angry rants

YOU MUST CHOOSE!

Would you rather...

battle to the death 30 parakeets
OR
5 possessed watermelons?

Would you rather...

have to mitigate a cock-block by President Obama
OR
Brad Pitt?

Would you rather...

find out your real father is a serial rapist in jail
OR
Glenn Beck?

YOU MUST CHOOSE!

Would you rather...

have a minstrel
OR
a butler?

Would you rather...

go on a mythical quest with a wizard fresh out of rehab
OR
an anti-Semitic elf ranger?

YOU MUST CHOOSE!

Would you rather...

be raised by wolves
OR
by Paula Abdul?

Would you rather...

have the ghost of Freud as your therapist
OR
have the ghost of George Washington Carver as your personal chef?
Things to consider: winning the science fair, peanut pie, peanut butter-covered peanuts, peanut smoothies, peanut forks

YOU MUST CHOOSE!

Would you rather...

French-kiss Liza Minnelli **OR** a bowl of sliced jalapeño peppers?

your aunt **OR** a pile of fish hooks?

the inside of a bowling shoe and ball **OR** (insert the ugliest or most disgusting person you know)?

Would you rather...

that your house was designed by Dr. Seuss
OR
M.C. Escher?

YOU MUST CHOOSE!

Would you rather...

your dreams were written by Judd Apatow
OR
James Cameron?

Would you rather...

have a political roundtable interview/discussion with Joe Biden, Sinbad, and Stone Cold Steve Austin
OR
Scott Baio, former Pakistani president President Pervez Musharraf, and Kendra Wilkinson?

YOU MUST CHOOSE!

Would you rather be Facebook friends with...

Spock **OR** Yoda?

an insanely rapidly status-updating Flash **OR** an Apache Chief who brags often about the tail he gets?

Wolverine **OR** Optimus Prime?

Things to consider: "Feeling good after eating a muffin, I am"; "Today I am feeling N/A?"

Would you rather...

share a bottle of whiskey with Vladimir Putin

OR

Robin Williams?

YOU MUST CHOOSE!

Would you rather...

follow the channeled Twitter of the ghost of Socrates
OR
Groucho Marx?

Would you rather battle in the water...

3 manatees **OR** 300 flounder?

20,000 guppies **OR** 1 swordfish?

5 beavers **OR** Aquaman while he is busy doing his taxes?

YOU MUST CHOOSE!

As you try to court a lady, who would you rather have hiding in the bushes feeding you lines like Cyrano de Bergerac...

Shakespeare **OR** Snoop Dogg?

Dennis Miller **OR** Charles Barkley?

Rocco Siffredi **OR** the Snausages mascot?

YOU MUST CHOOSE!

If you could travel through time, would you rather...

"pants" Benito Mussolini during a speech
OR
moon Joseph Stalin?

If you could travel through time, would you rather...

play Truth or Dare with all of the U.S. presidents
OR
play dodgeball against an array of conquistadors?
Things to consider: Who's the ugliest chick Chester A. Arthur nailed?; beaming Hernando Cortez in the nuts

YOU MUST CHOOSE!

If you could travel through time, would you rather...

play beer pong with the founding fathers
OR
go surfing with the ancient Greek philosophers?

Would you rather...

go to a strip bar with the nine Supreme Court justices
OR
go to a Supreme Court trial with nine strippers?

YOU MUST CHOOSE!

Which one of these people would you most want to slip some LSD?

Senator John McCain before a debate?

NBC News host Brian Williams before a broadcast?

your math teacher before class?

your boss before a presentation?

an endangered white rhinoceros?

Would you rather...

be followed everywhere by a police detective watching your every step
OR
a panhandling mummy?

YOU MUST CHOOSE!

For a night on the town, who would you rather have as your wingman?

Babe the talking pig?

Chad Ochocinco?

Pat Sajak?

Snarf from *The ThunderCats*?

Triumph the Insult Comic Dog?

Ghostface Killah from the Wu-Tang Clan?

YOU MUST CHOOSE!

Would you rather have an entourage of...

giggling, prepubescent teens **OR** corrupt Turkish politicians?

stoned surfers **OR** forlorn rodeo clowns?

a pack of raccoons **OR** day laborers?

Would you rather...

spend a year in a space station with Britney Spears in a crazy phase **OR**

a sleazy, always-hitting-on-you Count Chocula?

YOU MUST CHOOSE!

Would you rather...

share a spliff with the Dalai Lama **OR** Einstein?

Gandhi **OR** Gandalf?

your next door neighbors **OR** your teachers?

Would you rather...

fight to the death a grizzly bear **OR** 3 vampire IRS workers?

20 hostile soccer moms **OR** 6 hostile NASCAR dads?

a ninja who is looking for his keys **OR** a severely motion-sick mixed martial artist?

YOU MUST CHOOSE!

Would you rather...

fight 10 two-year-olds **OR** two 10-year-olds?

a 70-year-old **OR** 70 one-year-olds?

a 300-pound 12-year-old **OR** a 120-pound 30-year-old?

Who would you rather have as your prison cellmate?

Paris Hilton **OR** Martha Stewart?

Rush Limbaugh **OR** Carrot Top?

a really bad aspiring rap artist **OR** a dick-ish deaf dude?

YOU MUST CHOOSE!

Would you rather have to carpool to school every morning with...

Michael Moore **OR** three of the *Real Housewives of New Jersey*?

Genghis Khan **OR** Khan from *Star Trek*?

(insert most annoying person you know) **OR** (insert grossest person you know)?

Who would you rather have on your Pictionary team?

Picasso **OR** the UPS commercial guy?

YOU MUST CHOOSE!

Would you rather DJ a morning talk radio show with...

Joan Rivers **OR** Alan Greenspan?

Ricky Gervais **OR** Adam Carolla?

a lowbrow Paul Bunyan **OR** a strangely arch-conservative Johnny Appleseed?

Would you rather...

fight a creature with the body of a jaguar and the head of a cow
OR
fight a creature with the body of a horse and the head of Phil Mickelson?

YOU MUST CHOOSE!

Would you rather...

only be able to date psychiatric inmates **OR** reality show contestants?

Appalachian snake charmers **OR** Harlem Globetrotters?

close-up magicians **OR** secret agents?

Would you rather...

receive a lap dance from your sister
OR
your mother?

YOU MUST CHOOSE!

Would you rather...

share a camping tent with a PMS-ing Barbara Boxer
OR
an extremely flirtatious otter?

Would you rather...

be high school chemistry lab partners with Bill Nye the Science Guy
OR
have Boba Fett on your school's volleyball team?

Would you rather...

have Dr. Phil as your personal life coach
OR
have Orko from *He-Man* as your comic relief sidekick?

YOU MUST CHOOSE!

Would you rather...

have to share an office with Sharon Osbourne
OR
have to share toothbrushes with Gene Shalit?

You are a cannibal. Would you rather...

eat a lightly sautéed Megan Fox with braised vegetables and a white wine sauce
OR
a spicy Texas-barbecued Rachel McAdams?

YOU MUST CHOOSE!

Would you rather have your karaoke partner be...

Jason Mraz **OR** Jack Johnson?

George W. Bush's daughters **OR** his parents?

Iranian president Mahmoud Ahmadinejad **OR** Chewbacca?

YOU MUST CHOOSE!

Would you rather have a rare schizophrenia where you become convinced you are...

Xena the Warrior Princess **OR** Mario from Super Mario Bros?

the world's sexiest accountant **OR** a rhythm gymnastic gold medalist mid-routine?

a glass of orange juice afraid it will spill itself **OR** the lint in the lint filter of a dryer?

YOU MUST CHOOSE!

Would you rather...

be haunted by the ghost of Ike Turner

OR

constantly get drunk-dialed by Federal Reserve Chairman Ben Bernanke?

Would you rather...

have to ride around on a lazy burro

OR

a sweaty Al Sharpton?

Would you rather...

battle 50 penguins

OR

500 sentient wallets?

YOU MUST CHOOSE!

CHAPTER TEN

WOULD YOU RATHER...?
FOR WOMEN

Just because you are the fairer sex, doesn't mean you can't answer foul questions. Enjoy these questions that are strong enough for a man, but PH-balanced for a woman.[1]

---

[1] Is that still a thing?

Would you rather...

be able to inflate your breasts
OR
deflate your stomach?

Would you rather...

have sex with any ex of Lindsay Lohan's
OR
Paris Hilton's?

Would you rather...

never have to take the Pill again
OR
never menstruate again?

YOU MUST CHOOSE!

Would you rather...

have sex for five straight hours but only once a month
OR
every day but only for 30 seconds?

Would you rather...

give up lube
OR
vibrators?

Would you rather...

your orgasms sound like screeching cats
OR
your voice, but through Auto Tune?

YOU MUST CHOOSE!

Would you rather hook up with...

Gerard Butler **OR** Sam Worthington?

Colin Firth **OR** Hugh Grant?

Tiger Woods **OR** T-Pain?

Would you rather...

have a three-way with your boyfriend and best friend
OR
two strangers you found on Craigslist?

YOU MUST CHOOSE!

Would you rather...

gush tears when you're aroused
OR
have your hair stand on end?

Would you rather have:

one night with Johnny Depp?

orgasms on command for the next six months?

$1 million?

YOU MUST CHOOSE!

195

Would you rather...

have heels that can lower into flats
OR
a weightless purse?

Would you rather...

be able to will anything to fit exactly as you want it to
OR
be able to change the dressing-room light from gross neon
to a flattering glow?

Would you rather...

get a shopping spree of $1,000 at Marc Jacobs
OR
$10,000 at Target?

YOU MUST CHOOSE!

Would you rather...

be able to predict fashion trends a season in advance
OR
magically update your wardrobe to reflect current styles every year?

Would you rather...

have to sew your own clothes
OR
cut your own hair?

YOU MUST CHOOSE!

Whose style would you rather have?

Chloe Sevigny **OR** Katie Holmes?

Victoria Beckham **OR** Anna Wintour?

Kim Kardashian **OR** Snooki?

Would you rather...

make men spend a day in 4-inch heels
OR
thongs?

YOU MUST CHOOSE!

Would you rather...

have a closet the size of your bedroom, filled with designer items
OR
never have to diet again?

Would you rather...

have armpit hair that grows at 100 times the normal rate
OR
toenails that do the same thing?

Would you rather...

wax your entire body
OR
shave your head?

YOU MUST CHOOSE!

Would you rather...

have a personal masseuse
OR
personal shopper/stylist?

Would you rather...

wake up with coiffed hair
OR
minty breath?

Would you rather...

be able to get ready in five minutes
OR
have hair impervious to wind, rain and humidity?

YOU MUST CHOOSE!

Would you rather...

have legs that never needed shaving
OR
feet that pedicure themselves?

Would you rather...

be able to shrink zits with mind control
OR
have a fairy with tiny tweezers to pluck your eyebrows?

YOU MUST CHOOSE!

199

Would you rather...

legally change your name to Veronica Vulvatron
OR
Mons Pubis McGee?

Would you rather...

be able to shrink your exes' penises
OR
make their girlfriends uglier?

YOU MUST CHOOSE!

Would you rather...

have the ability to make your boss lose an erection

OR

get an erection?

Would you rather...

find the world's most perfect man, only to discover he has a mistress on the side

OR

that he has copious back hair and back acne?

Would you rather...

have a private jet and pilot at your disposal

OR

a brawny, dopey assistant whose only job is to pleasure you?

YOU MUST CHOOSE!

Would you rather...

have breasts that hang down to your waist
OR
have an ass that hangs down to your knees?

Would you rather...

be able to have consequence-free sex in any public place
OR
have condoms that actually do not affect sensation?

YOU MUST CHOOSE!

Would you rather...

get twelve weeks vacation per year
OR
only work three days a week?

Would you rather...

out-earn your partner
OR
make less but receive lots of extravagant gifts?

Would you rather...

time travel to live as a Suffragette
OR
flapper?

YOU MUST CHOOSE!

Would you rather...

go on a blind date with a gorgeous but dumb guy
OR
an ugly guy with a perfect penis?

Would you rather...

act in porn
OR
allow your normal sex life to be streamed on YouTube?

Would you rather...

have a home out of an interior design magazine
OR
a wardrobe out of *Vogue*?

YOU MUST CHOOSE!

Would you rather...

only need two hours of sleep per night
OR
500 calories per day?

Would you rather...

achieve world peace
OR
have perfect hair?

YOU MUST CHOOSE!

Would you rather...

never physically age past 30
OR
never emotionally age past 15?

Would you rather...

pose naked for an art class
OR
go to the beach in a thong for a whole day?

Would you rather...

blink 100 times per minute
OR
queef every 40 seconds?

YOU MUST CHOOSE!

CHAPTER ELEVEN

WOULD YOU RATHER...? FOR MEN

Gadgets! Babes! Beer! Porn! Bathroom Humor! Megan Fox! BBQ! Tits!
Movies! Ass! Analysis of Neo-Marxist Dialectical Materialsim! Red Meat!
Classic Movie Quotes! More Tits! Not Much Reading! iPad! Cyborgs!
Lions! Tigers! Bears (not the hairy, burly, gay type!) Taffy! Sex! Slutty
Celeb Pics! Uh... Rookie Cards!... hmm... running out of gas here...
Bagels?... No... Did we say "Tits" yet?

Would you rather...

set off a mousetrap with your penis
OR
a bear trap with your leg?

Would you rather...

block a punt with your nuts
OR
your face?

YOU MUST CHOOSE!

Would you... have sex with Carrie Fisher now to be able to relive time and have sex with Carrie Fisher when you were 15 and she was in *Return of the Jedi*?

Would you... have sex with Kendra Wilkinson if you have to spend two weeks hanging out with her all day long first? What if you could have sex first and then had to spend two weeks hanging out afterwards (with no more sex)?

YOU MUST CHOOSE!

Would you rather...

have an app that indicates the ovulation and STD status of potential one-night stands

OR

the number of times she's been dumped for "being crazy?"

Would you rather...

motorboat Scarlett Johansson's boobs

OR

Shakira's butt?

Would you rather...

have sex with Taylor Swift, swiftly

OR

Jenna Haze, hazily?

YOU MUST CHOOSE!

Who would make the best lesbian porn?

Cylons number six and nine from *Battlestar Galactica*?

Ginger and Mary Ann from *Gilligan's Island*?

Pocahontas and the chick from Disney's *Aladdin*?

the *Gossip Girl* cast **OR** the *True Blood* cast?

Playmate centerfolds of 1976 **OR** female *X-Men* characters?

YOU MUST CHOOSE!

Would you rather...

every time you get an erection, you get a nosebleed and vice-versa
OR
lose all sexual inhibition in the presence of nutmeg?

Would you rather...

have an erection for 3 months straight
OR
your wife/girlfriend be on her period for 3 months straight?

YOU MUST CHOOSE!

Would you rather have sex with....

Elizabeth Banks **OR** Rachel McAdams?

Naomi Watts **OR** Anna Faris?

Emmanuelle Chriqui if she was wearing Rec Specs **OR** Keeley Hazell if she was wearing gag glasses with a moustache?

Denise Milani if she were completely flat-chested and had a dumpy ass **OR** Angela Lansbury if she were a 36DD-22-34?

YOU MUST CHOOSE!

Would you rather...

see your girlfriend in a sex video on the web
OR
see your mom in a *Girls Gone Wild* tape?

Would you rather...

stick you penis in a wasp's nest
OR
in (insert disgusting acquaintance)'s mouth?

Would you rather...

that all women in the world were required to return phone calls,
no matter what
OR
that all women in the world had vaginas that recorded high scores
like video games, so you enter your initials afterward and try
to break your records?

YOU MUST CHOOSE!

Would you rather...

be caught by your mom masturbating
OR
catch your mom masturbating?
Dad?
Aunt?
Grandfather?
Dog?
Ben Kingsley?

Would you rather...

watch *Twilight* 20 times in a row with your wife/girlfriend
OR
eat 5 sticks of butter?

YOU MUST CHOOSE!

Would you rather...

split a 12-pack with Jimmy Kimmel
OR
Donald Rumsfeld?

Would you rather...

play 18 holes with Tiger Woods
OR
DP 18 holes with Tiger Woods and his mistresses?
Things to consider: playing in the rough, ball-washers, other obvious golf jokes

YOU MUST CHOOSE!

Which porno would you most want to watch, imagining what the plot would be?

The Fast and Bicurious

Womb Raider

Schindler's Fist

The Incredible Bulge — (penis turns green and rips through clothes when excited)

Semento (told backwards from ejaculation all the way to putting clothes back on)

The Firm

YOU MUST CHOOSE!

Would you rather...

have a zip-up change purse scrotum
OR
have a scrotum that blows up and expands into a beanbag chair?

Would you rather...

have an elastic scrotum that you can use as a nunchuck-like weapon
to fight crime
OR
one made of that stress ball material that you can squeeze
to reduce stress?

Note: This page reprinted with permission from William Shakespeare's *The Tempest*.

YOU MUST CHOOSE!

Would you... want to marry a creature who was half person/half couch?

Would you... attend a full season's games of the nearest WNBA team for a threesome with Erin Andrews and Anna Kournikova?

Would you... suckle from a nursing cow to suckle from Salma Hayek?

YOU MUST CHOOSE!

DATE, MARRY, SCREW

Which would you date, which would you marry, and which would you screw?

Olivia Munn, Kathy Griffin, a mythical Griffin?

Jennifer Aniston, Courtney Cox, Megatron?
Things to consider: Aniston's legs, Cox's eyes, Megatron's desire for world domination and utter annihilation of the Autobots

Would you rather...

titty-fuck Jessica Rabbit
OR
fin-fuck the Little Mermaid?

YOU MUST CHOOSE!

Would you rather have sex with...

Danica Patrick **OR** Venus Williams?

an Olympic gymnast **OR** an Olympic figure skater?

tennis star Maria Sharapova grunting like she does when she plays **OR** hottie golf star Kim Hall as quiet as she is when she golfs?

a beach volleyball player covered in sand **OR** a pro bowler who celebrates upon orgasm like they would when they bowl a strike?
Things to consider: bowler's proclivity for instituting the Shocker, keeping score

Would you rather...

have your testicles set on a tee and hit by a five year old with a Wiffle bat

OR

have your testicles lowered between bumpers on a pinball machine?

YOU MUST CHOOSE!

Would you rather...

bang the *Sex in the City* characters in increasing order of sluttiness
OR
your choice of two panelists on *The View?*

Would you rather...

have sex with Lady Gaga
OR
with a few of her stage outfits?

YOU MUST CHOOSE!

Would you... screw Amy Winehouse in order to have her become sober and healthy?

Would you... toss the salad of your offensive linemen to be quarterback for a game in the NFL?

Would you... try to continue having sex with a very hot drunk woman if she threw up a little during sex? What would you say?

YOU MUST CHOOSE!

Would you rather...

plant an herb garden with Mandy Moore
OR
ride a freight train with Katherine Heigl?

Would you rather...

have group sex with the Pussycat Dolls
OR
the Spice Girls in their prime?

Would you rather...

have sex with Jennifer Lopez with H1N1
OR
let Jennifer Garner give you butterfly kisses with pinkeye?

YOU MUST CHOOSE!

Would you rather...

have Wolverine-type retractable claws made of penises
OR
not?

Would you rather...

go to a bachelor party thrown by Kubla Kahn
OR
by Jabba the Hut?

Things to consider: the Mongol Horde is a potential sausage fest, keg stands with Boba Fett

Would you rather...

have sex with Jennifer Hudson
OR
pop Megan Fox's back zits?

YOU MUST CHOOSE!

While you're having sex, would you rather your partner scream out...

"Make love to me." **OR** "Fuck me harder!!!"

"Have you ever done this before?" **OR** "Allahu Akbar!"?

"Treat me like a whore!" **OR** "Kibbles and bits! Kibbles and bits! I've got to get me some kibbles and bits!"?

Would you rather...

have one clean shot to hit on Mila Kunis
OR
one clean shot to the face of Ryan Seacrest?

YOU MUST CHOOSE!

Would you rather...

have a detachable penis

OR

a penis that vibrates on command?

Would you rather...

lick Courtney Love's vibrator

OR

Tom Selleck's moustache?

Would you rather...

eat two live baby hamsters

OR

have sex with (insert disgusting acquaintance)?

YOU MUST CHOOSE!

CHAPTER TWELVE **12**

GROSS —
GROVER CLEVELAND

We are trying a little experiment with this chapter. This chapter is segmented by alphabetical order. Here you'll find questions about the "gross," then we'll move on to the "grotesque," and finally, the chapter will culminate with questions concerning "Grover Cleveland."

Would you rather...

groom a volatile gorilla
OR
groom the dingleberries from Michael Moore's ass hair?

Would you rather...

be climbing up the ladder and feel something splatter
OR
be sliding into first and feel something burst?
Things to consider: diarrhea, uh-uh, diarrheah.

YOU MUST CHOOSE!

Would you rather...

throw up right into a fan
OR
lick the dead bugs off of a car windshield?

Would you rather...

take it in the crapper
OR
on the crapper?

Would you rather...

have a beetle crawl in and around your mouth for two minutes
OR
have an inch worm slowly inch up your left nostril and out your right nostril?

YOU MUST CHOOSE!

Would you rather...

drink a pint of lukewarm asparagus pee
OR
16 ounces of chilled ball sweat?

Would you rather...

use a live possum as a pillow each night
OR
use a pile of rolled-up dirty diapers?

YOU MUST CHOOSE!

Would you rather...

have a tongue made of hair
OR
hair made of tongues?

Would you rather...

drink a glass of ten-month-old-milkshake complete with green chunky goodness
OR
eat a bowl of rat tails n' cheese?

YOU MUST CHOOSE!

Would you rather...

sleep nightly in pajamas made of dentists' used gauze
OR
have to reach into a horse's ass every time you want the key
to your home?

Would you rather...

feel compelled to greet people by licking their feet
OR
by intensely smelling their armpits?

YOU MUST CHOOSE!

Would you rather...

have zits that pop by themselves, squirting as much goo as there is in a ketchup packet

OR

have zits that crawl all over your face like little ants?

Would you rather...

get poison ivy under your eyelid

OR

on your tongue?

Would you rather...

eat chocolate-covered cockroaches

OR

deep-fried roadkill?

YOU MUST CHOOSE!

Would you rather...

eat a cow-eye-and-cricket shish kabob marinated in camel spit
OR
a salad of giant moth wings tossed in dog slobber dressing?

Would you rather...

get a hickey from each of your grandparents
OR
give them each one?

Would you rather...

get a mayonnaise enema
OR
eat a piece of bull-semen-iced angelfood cake?

YOU MUST CHOOSE!

Would you rather...

hold a slug on your tongue for two hours
OR
get a bee sting on your sphincter?

Would you rather...

eat a regurgitated cat hairball
OR
pasta boiled in used toilet water?

YOU MUST CHOOSE!

Would you rather...

lick clean the inside of a horse's nostril
OR
have a horse lick the insides of your nostril?

Would you rather...

get sprayed by a skunk in the mouth
OR
by Franco Harris in the ear?

Would you rather...

play basketball against a gross, flabby, hairy, shirtless, sweaty old dude
OR
play tackle football against a 300 pounder?

YOU MUST CHOOSE!

Would you rather...

have your body hair suddenly turn into fleas
OR
have your saliva suddenly turn into glue?

Would you rather...

eat a cotton candy that turns out to be a cocoon full of caterpillars
OR
that turned out to be an old man's whitened pubic hair?

YOU MUST CHOOSE!

Would you rather...

have bloodworms for facial hair

OR

use facial hair for fishing bait? (work in progress)

Would you rather...

after sneezing, use a piece of used tissue

OR

just use your shirt?

YOU MUST CHOOSE!

Would you rather...

have projectile vomit
OR
have projectile diarrhea?

Would you rather...

have an infestation of bedbugs
OR
bed Larry Kings?

Would you rather...

lose control of your bowels upon orgasm
OR
vice-versa?

YOU MUST CHOOSE!

Would you rather...

have your horror-movie death involve a chainsaw **OR** a meat hook?

ice pick **OR** toothpicks?

shoehorn **OR** Ivan Lendl?

Would you rather...

be thrown up on while giving
OR
receiving oral sex?

YOU MUST CHOOSE!

Would you rather...

wear used urinal cake ear muffs

OR

brush with smegma toothpaste?

Would you rather...

drop a Mentos in a glass of Diet Coke and immediately take a swig

OR

have an enema of the same?

Would you rather...

drink a maggot smoothie

OR

bathe in the thick gooey fat drained from Hollywood actress's liposuction treatments?

YOU MUST CHOOSE!

Would you rather...

have a lawnmower run over a cow patty and spatter you with its smelly chopped-up bits

OR

have to clean out a soiled hamster's cage with your bare hands?

Would you rather...

breathe through your navel

OR

through your butt?

Things to consider: snorkeling, wearing baggy pants to give you some breathing room, if you have an outie or innie

YOU MUST CHOOSE!

Would you rather...

shove a straw into a big blister and suck away
OR
eat a sherbet-sized scoop of ear wax?

Would you rather...

eat raw cow stomach
OR
stomach 500 cow farts in a row, standing 2 inches behind the cow?

Would you rather...

eat a Twinkie filled with human blood
OR
eat a Nutty Buddy rolled in dingleberries?

YOU MUST CHOOSE!

If you were Grover Cleveland, would you rather...

intervene in the Pullman Strike of 1894 to keep the railroads moving, thereby angering labor unions nationwide

OR

support the gold standard and oppose free silver thereby alienating the agrarian wing of the Democratic Party?

Would you rather...

be haunted by the ghosts of Grover Cleveland's appointed Supreme Court justices Lucius Q.C. Lamar and Melville Fuller

OR

have nightmares where you are being attacked by Grover Cleveland's mustache?

YOU MUST CHOOSE!

Would you... have a three-way with Grover Cleveland and vice-president Adlai Stevenson to reverse their stance on the 15th amendment, guaranteeing rights for African Americans?

YOU MUST CHOOSE!

CHAPTER THIRTEEN

RANDOM/"RANDOM"

If you like the weird, "random" questions full of obscure references, mad-libby nonsense and strange juxtapositions, then this chapter is for you. If, on the other hand, you prefer more straightforward mainstream material, please turn to page 184. Of another book.

Would you rather...

have perpetual helium voice

OR

shake your head knowingly and say "Old School!" after anything
a person you meet for the first time says during conversation?

Would you rather...

have a rare condition where you assume all police officers you see
are coming after you

OR

coming on to you?

Would you rather...

no matter what, always be wearing a leopard skin and holding a club

OR

no matter what, always be holding a knife and wearing
blood-soaked clothing?

Things to consider: walks in the park, grocery shopping,
parent teacher conferences

YOU MUST CHOOSE!

Would you rather...

have phantom phone syndrome where you constantly think your phone vibrates even when it doesn't

OR

have phantom yarmulke syndrome?

Would you rather...

be a brilliant songwriter, but only get inspired after making out with former Secretary of State Madeleine Albright

OR

have keen foresight about the stock market, but only while fondling a head of lettuce in public?

YOU MUST CHOOSE!

Would you rather...

have eyelids that are always flipped up

OR

have all of your skin be wrinkly, scraggly-haired scrotum skin?

Would you rather...

have a rare speech impediment where your lips and voice are out of sync like a '70s kung fu movie

OR

have an air horn blast the second you are not sitting with perfect posture?

Would you rather...

wink flirtatiously after every sentence

OR

be mentally sound in every way, except completely unable to use faucets?

YOU MUST CHOOSE!

Would you rather...

have to solve a SuDoKu before being able to open the refrigerator

OR

before being allowed to go home from work, have to draw 100 high-fives from different strangers?

Would you rather...

only be able to urinate while reciting the pledge of allegiance

OR

have an acid flashback of the Vietnam War anytime anyone says "facetious"?

YOU MUST CHOOSE!

Would you rather...

have to legally change your name to "Lelsdy" **OR** "Trongar"?

"The (insert your name here)" **OR** "(insert your name here) of the Mountain People"?

the sound of a glass shattering **OR** the smell of vanilla?

Would you rather...

only be able to communicate with people via singing telegram
OR
singing anagram?

YOU MUST CHOOSE!

Would you rather...

have a rectum that can sing like Frank Sinatra

OR

a vagina with the sardonic wit of Beatrice Arthur?

Would you rather...

have to drink everything via keg stand

OR

from a thimble-sized glass?

YOU MUST CHOOSE!

Would you rather...

stare fixedly at people's nostrils when speaking to them
OR
sob uncontrollably anytime you use the ATM?

Would you rather...

have to get a new plastic surgery procedure every month
OR
have to get a new tattoo every day?

YOU MUST CHOOSE!

Would you rather...

only be able to talk to the opposite sex in '70s jive
OR
like Gollum from *Lord of the Rings*?

Would you rather...

have the ability to telekinetically control anyone's arms
OR
anyone's hair?

Would you rather...

burp fireflies
OR
fart smooth jazz?

YOU MUST CHOOSE!

Would you rather...

never be able take off your underwear
OR
a catcher's mitt?

Would you rather...

in all photographs, appear as Erik Estrada
OR
uncontrollably shriek every time you see argyle?

YOU MUST CHOOSE!

Would you rather...

have 8 ears **OR** 36 nostrils?

10 eyes **OR** 24 fingers?

400 lips **OR** 8000 toes?

Would you rather...

recite famous historical speeches in your sleep
OR
perform various swim strokes in your sleep?

YOU MUST CHOOSE!

Would you rather have sex with the hybrid...

Linda LaVin Diesel **OR** Sarah Jessica Parker Posey?

Rep. Barney Frank Sinatra **OR** Lil' Kim Jong Il?

Selma Blair Underwood **OR** Bruce Willis McGahee?

Angie Harmon Killebrew **OR** Ashley Judd Nelson?

Kurt Russell Brand **OR** Ricky Martin Lawrence?

Now decide which hybrid you would rather have sex with.

YOU MUST CHOOSE!

Would you rather...

be completely unable to detect sarcasm
OR
be the totally awesome reader that we *really* care about even though this is the fifteenth year of writing this stuff that doesn't bore us at all any more?

Would you rather be able to move with your mind...

bowling pins **OR** motorcycles?

cauliflower **OR** worms?

silverware **OR** chalk?
Things to consider: how would you use your powers?

YOU MUST CHOOSE!

Would you rather...

speak as if you are always out of breath
OR
speak as if you were using an auto tuner (the thing that makes singers sound robotic)?

Would you rather...

when eating, shift into slow motion
OR
speak like a wise Native American chief whenever you're chilly?

Would you rather...

sneeze a blast of shotgun pellets
OR
always look like you are crying with tons of makeup smearing?
Things to consider: the angle of your head when sneezing, the kick-back of a sneeze, kissing

YOU MUST CHOOSE!

Would you rather...

not be able to tell the difference between keys and Q-tips
OR
guns and celery?

Would you rather...

have tennis ball-sized eyeballs
OR
coffee mug-sized nostrils?

YOU MUST CHOOSE!

Would you rather...

be unable to stop from tackling anyone over 75-years-old
OR
grow a bushy beard every day on a different part of your body?
Things to consider: visiting a retirement home, knee-beards, foot beards, forehead beards

Would you rather...

have extra eyeballs in the palms of your hands
OR
detachable ears that you can leave anywhere and work
like walkie-talkies?

Would you rather...

have a goatee (ring of hair) around each eye
OR
have earlobes that connect under your chin?

YOU MUST CHOOSE!

Would you rather...

have poppy-seeded skin

OR

have asparagus for hair?

Would you rather...

say the word "whitefish" every other word as in: "Hi whitefish, how whitefish, have whitefish you whitefish been?"

OR

have a strange condition where anytime you walk into a room, dozens of pickles fall on your head?

YOU MUST CHOOSE!

Would you rather...

only be able to enter rooms by Kool-Aid-man-style wall crashes
OR
only be able to exit rooms by jumping through a window as if fleeing a burning building?

Would you rather...

have baby-sized feet
OR
baby-sized hands?
Things to consider: sports, writing, toppling, finding shoes

Would you rather...

be able to shoot mustard from your eyes
OR
be able to extend one eyeball up, out and around corners like a submarine periscope?

YOU MUST CHOOSE!

Would you rather...

have glow-in-the-dark poops
OR
dimes for boogers?

Would you rather...

have to battle a blindfolded Bengal tiger **OR** 600 yipping poodles?

a 5x scale Betty White **OR** a 1/5x Chuck Norris?

your own left hand **OR** your own right foot?

Would you rather...

all family functions and celebrations be held in an ATM vestibule
OR
catered exclusively by the bourbon chicken free sample guy
from the mall food court?

YOU MUST CHOOSE!

Would you rather...

be getting busy with someone for the first time, and as you take their pants off, you see they have the largest amount of pubic hair you have ever seen
OR
you see a crotch tattoo of Matlock?

Would you rather have all your future dreams consist of...

being naked in high school **OR** of taking a test you forgot to study for?

being surrounded by lingerie-wearing Richard Nixon clones **OR** playing Parcheesi with a temperamental Charles Barkley?

being trapped in a passionless marriage to Eli Whitney **OR** being sexually harassed by Oliver Wendell Holmes?

YOU MUST CHOOSE!

Would you rather...

look like this

OR

look like this?

YOU MUST CHOOSE!

CHAPTER  FOURTEEN

WHAT WOULD YOU BE?

How to Use This Chapter

Game 1: I Am Thinking of Someone We All Know. This is a way to use this chapter as a group game. One player thinks of someone who everybody in the group knows: a friend, a coworker, an enemy, a teacher, etc. This is the "name on the table." Other players take turns reading a randomly selected page of questions from this chapter. The player who is thinking of someone answers each question as if he were that person. After every page, have a player guess who you are thinking of. Optional: If you want, you can all write down a bunch of people you know on scraps of paper, turn them over, and have the answerer pull a name from the pile.

Game 2: Conversation. Pretty simple. Read a question and answer it as yourself. If there is a group of you, everybody should answer the question. Suggest your own answers for what you think others are and discuss why. See who agrees and who disagrees. Debate. Deliberate. Arm-wrestle. Think about other people you know (your friends, family, bosses, etc.) and what they would be. When the conversation fades into silence and awkward stares—you guessed it—it's time to move on to the next question.

Game 3: Celebrity. Go back a page. Reread the directions for Game 1, but substitute "celebrity" for "someone who everybody in the group knows."

Game 4: Ninja Strike. Find a horde of bandits marauding caravans. Train in the martial arts, specializing in book warfare. Fashion this book into a throwing star or other deadly piece of weaponry. Defeat marauders.

If you were a **company**, what would you be?

If you were **something that goes in the mouth**, what would you be?

If you were a **cooking technique** (grilling, broiling, slow-cook, etc.), what would you be?

If you were any **palindrome** (race car, mom, dad, etc.), what would you be?

YOU MUST CHOOSE!

YOUR TRUE CHARACTER

If you were a **character** from *Harry Potter*,
who would you be?

If you were a **character** from *Lost*,
who would you be?

If you were a **character** from *True Blood*,
who would you be?

If you were a **character** from *Sex and the City*, who would you be?

If you were a **character** from *Grey's Anatomy*, who would you be?

YOU MUST CHOOSE!

If you were a Starbucks order, what would you be?
(Give a detailed order.)
Things to consider: Are you decaf? Skim? Size? Iced? Latte?

If you were a jungle animal, what would you be?

If you were a kind of massage, what would you be?
(Demonstrate if needed.)
Things to consider: Would you be forceful? Gentle? An erotic massage? A neurotic massage?

QUESTION OF CHARACTER

Would you ever give or receive a "happy ending" massage? A happy beginning? A melancholy middle?

YOU MUST CHOOSE!

275

If you were a **tree**, what would you be?

If you were a **coin**, which coin would you be?

If you were a **piece of gardening equipment**, what would you be?

If you were any **alien as depicted in science fiction**, what would you be?
Things to consider: the ferocious creature in *Alien*, the seemingly benign but ultimately evil reptiles from *V*, Jawas, the ultralogical *Star Trek* super-race susceptible to being defeated by paradox.

YOU MUST CHOOSE!

SETTING THE BAR

If you were a type of bar, what would you be? Describe your:

Décor and lighting?

Clientele? What sort of conversations do they have? Are there fights?

What do you serve? What sort of neighborhood are you located in?

What music is playing? Any other details?

What are you named?

YOU MUST CHOOSE!

If you were a **character from** *Peanuts*, who would you be?

Things to consider: Are you balding? Do you neglect your personal hygiene to the point of being a health hazard? Do you need a security blanket? Are you a Butch lesbian? Do you hold things out for people and suddenly take them away?

If you were a **foreign language**, what would you be?

If you were an **obscene gesture**, what would you be? (Demonstration optional.)

If you were a **period in history**, which period would you be?

YOU MUST CHOOSE!

WHO IS THIS FAMOUS PERSON?

If he were an **animal**, he might be a hyena. Though a few would claim he is a lion.

If he were a **weapon**, he'd be a whip or maybe a Colt 45.

If he were a **tool**, he'd be a hammer.

If he were a **key on the keyboard**, detractors would say he'd be the Delete key. Supporters would say he's the Enter key.

If he were a **punctuation mark**, he'd be an exclamation mark.

Answer: George W. Bush

What Would You Be?

If you were a **road sign**, what would you be?

YOU MUST CHOOSE!

If you were a **reptile or amphibian**, what would you be?

If you were a **commercial slogan** ("Just Do It", "Sometimes you feel like a nut…", "I'm not gonna pay a lot for this muffler…", "Keeps on going and going and going…", etc.), what would you be?

If you were a **character from *Friends***, which would you be?

If you were an **over-the-counter medication**, what would you be?

Did you know?

*Matt LeBlanc has two club feet.**

*Not true.

YOU MUST CHOOSE!

WEB YOU.0

If you were a **website**, what would you be?

If you were a **download speed**, what would you be? Does your connection go out a lot?

If you were a **spider web**, what would you look like? Draw it. What if Charlotte from *Charlotte's Web* made a web to represent you?

QUESTION OF CHARACTER

If you started typing "po…" in a web browser, what is most likely to pop up from frequent use: popsugar.com, pornocentral.com, or polygonsrcool.net? Check your browser and see.

YOU MUST CHOOSE!

If you were a **Monopoly property** (Boardwalk, Baltic Avenue, etc.), what would you be?

If you were an **extinct animal**, what would you be?

If you were a **number between one and ten**, what number would you be?

Things to consider: What number gets laid the most? What number is the biggest asshole? What is the most beautiful number? The most mysterious? The most pelborp?

If you were an **item in the supermarket**, what would you be?

QUESTION OF CHARACTER

What are the **first five items** on your shopping list?

What would never be on it?

YOU MUST CHOOSE!

Are you...

Meat, chicken, or fish?

87, 89, or 93 gasoline?

Boxers, briefs, or nothing?

Firemen, police, or paramedics?

a shot, assist, or rebound?

YOU MUST CHOOSE!

If you were **something in a yard**, what would you be?

If you were **something in a mall**, what would you be?

If you were **something in Washington, D.C.**, what would you be?

If you were **something in the closet**, what would you be?

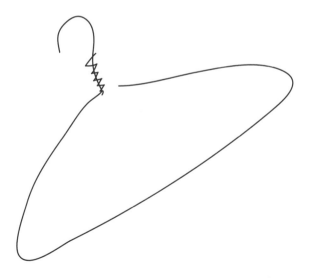

YOU MUST CHOOSE!

WHO'S THE BOSS?

If your boss were a **movie villain**, which one would he/she be?

If your boss were an **amusement park ride**, which one would he/she be?

If your boss were a **piece of email spam**, what would the subject line say?

If your boss were a **tourist attraction**, which would he/she be?

YOU MUST CHOOSE!

Are you …

a **consonant** or a **vowel**?

a **thrust** or a **parry**?

Bert or **Ernie**?

Dr. Jekyll or **Mr. Hyde**?

a **whisper** or a **shout**?

YOU MUST CHOOSE!

FANTASY FOOTBALL

If you were a **position in football**, what would you be?

If you were a **football play** (sack, touchdown, reverse, blocked punt, Hail Mary, etc.), which would you be? Bonus: Do the commentary of four downs that embody your life.

If you were an **NFL team**, what team would you be and why? Examples: A Bengal—good-looking uniform (body), ugly helmet (face).

If you were a **football penalty**, what would you be?

QUESTION OF CHARACTER

If you had to do a **post-touchdown celebration** that personifies you, what would you do? (Demonstrate it.)

YOU MUST CHOOSE!

If you were a **song from the early eighties**, what song would you be?

If you were a **cut of steak**, what cut would you be? How would you be cooked? Seasoned?

If you were a **sitcom character**, who would you be?

QUESTION OF CHARACTER

If you had an **original sitcom catchphrase**, what would it be? Some ideas: … "Uh, NO THANK YOU!"; "That's a little more info than I need to knooooowwwwwwwww!"; "Guess you had to be there"; "Indeeditron 2000!"; and "Sheeeeeyit!"

YOU MUST CHOOSE!

289

SUMPIN' SUMPIN'

If you were **something with wheels,** what would you be?

If you were **something with wings,** what would you be?

If you were **something on a farm,** what would you be?

If you were **something in the kitchen,** what would you be?

Things to consider: Can you think of an object that satisfies all of the above? If so, email the answer to info@wouldyourather.com, subject heading: "Too much time on my balls." So far, the best we have is a partially formed chicken in an egg (but no wheels).

YOU MUST CHOOSE!

If you were a **Disney character**, what would you be?

If you were a **gun**, what would you be?

If you were a **mythical creature**, what would you be?

If you were an **architectural style**, what would you be?

QUESTION OF CHARACTER

If *Disney on Ice* put on an **ice show of your life**, how would that go?

YOU MUST CHOOSE!

If you were a **mode of transportation**,
what would you be?

If you were an **email command**, what would you be?
Things to consider: reply, forward, delete, archive, send, keep as new

If you were a **store**, what would you be?

If you were a **magic spell**, what would you be?
Things to consider; invisibility, forcefield, fireball, freeze, levitate, turn to
stone, poison, prismatic lights, cure wounds.

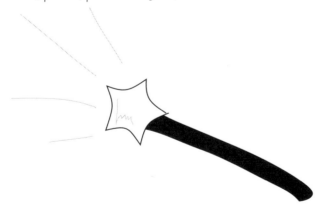

YOU MUST CHOOSE!

If you were a **disease**, what would you be?

If you were a **culture from history** (Aztec, Vikings, Cherokee, etc.), what would you be?

If you were a **bumper sticker**, what would you be?

If you were a **button on your TV remote**, what would you be?

YOU MUST CHOOSE!

20 STUPID QUESTIONS

Take a break from WWYB to play this game. If in a public place, pick someone you don't know, but that each of you can see. If not in a public place, think of a well-known celebrity or historical figure. Then play 20 questions, but use only these questions of conjecture. One player pick the person, the other ask. After asking/answering these questions, guess who the person is. Indeeditron 2000.

- Could you see this person secretly liking to be tied up and dominated?
- Does this person misspell "maintenance"?
- If this person was in a fight with John Larroquette, would they win?
- Is this person a farter?
- Does this person sing in the shower? On the toilet?
- Does he/she have a good voice?
- Does this person like penguins?
- Do these pants make my butt look big? My balls?

YOU MUST CHOOSE!

If you were a donut, what would you be? What if you were a doughnut?

If you were a president, who would you be?

If you were a decade, which decade would you be?

If you were a TV channel, what would you be?

Did you know?

John Quincy Adams was the world's first bisexual.*

*Not true.

YOU MUST CHOOSE!

If you were a kiss, what would you be?
(Demonstrate on your hand.)

If you were foreplay, what would you be?
(Demonstrate on your forearm.)

If you were a form of sexual intercourse,
what would you be? (Demonstrate on the throw pillow or
couch corner.)

QUESTION OF CHARACTER

What is the weirdest sexual dream you've
ever had?

YOU MUST CHOOSE!

If you were a beer, what would you be?

If you were an occupation, what would you be?

If you were a height, which one would you be?

If you were a drunken antic, what would you be?
Act it out.
Things to consider: being over-friendly, getting into a fight, dropping pants, talking too much like Loose Lips Schirtz.

YOU MUST CHOOSE!

If you were a **basketball shot**, what would you be? (Examples: short-range jump hook, two-handed tomahawk dunk, fade-away 3-pointer)? Does your shot go in?

If you were a **famous singer**, who would you be?

If you were a **school supply**, what would you be?

If you were a **dance style**, what would you be (tap, break-dancing, ballet, square-dancing, etc.)?

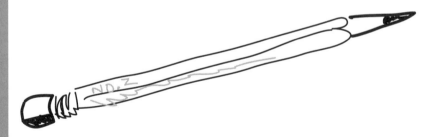

YOU MUST CHOOSE!

ACTING OUT

If you were a **talent show act**, what would it be?
(Demonstrate it.)

If you were a **'70s song**, which would it be?
(Sing it.)

If you were a **quote from a movie**, what would it be?
(Say it.)

If you were a **scene from a movie**, which would it be?
(Mime it.)

YOU MUST CHOOSE!

If you were a **street**, what would you be?

If you were a **fashion accessory**, what would you be?

If you were a **soda**, what would you be?

If you were a **classic arcade game character**, what would you be?

Things to consider: Are you a glutton that loves the thrill of the chase? Do you have a hero streak and a propensity to dodge barrels either literally or metaphorically? Are you prone to diagonal hopping and unidentifiably punctuated profanity?

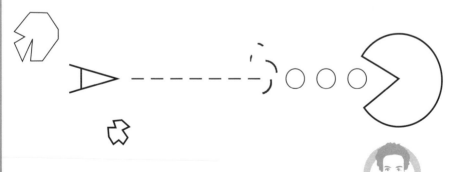

YOU MUST CHOOSE!

If you were a **fashion label**, which one would you be?

If you were a **restaurant chain**, which would you be?

If you were a **part of speech**, which would you be?

If you were a **spread that you put on bread**
(mayonnaise, margarine, peanut butter, Vegemite,
marshmallow fluff, etc.), what would you be?

YOU MUST CHOOSE!

CHAPTER 15 FIFTEEN

FANTASIES

Albert Einstein once said, "The gift of fantasy has meant more to me than my talent for absorbing positive knowledge." Consequently, Einstein was a profound and constant masturbator, which very few people realize. His productivity would have been twice what it was if he could manage to stave off his flooding fantasies. But we cannot deny the dreaming mind. As human beings, we must feed it. And so we present to you these choices in the far-off, far-out realms of fantasy. Choose wisely (unlike Einstein).

Would you rather...

be allowed to destroy Lego Land, pretending you are a giant monster

OR

be allowed to have a paintball war in your office?

Would you rather...

have Yoda as your personal bodyguard

OR

as your (or your child's) school guidance counselor?

Would you rather...

watch Britney Spears and Christina Aguilera in a UFC match-up

OR

watch Dick Cheney and Hillary Clinton?

YOU MUST CHOOSE!

Would you rather...

have a star on the Hollywood Walk of Fame
OR
have a deli sandwich named after you?

Would you rather...

be slapped by an ugly girl
OR
thrown up on by a hot girl?

Would you rather...

have an element on the periodic chart renamed after you
OR
have a new hit dance based on your movement style sweep the country?

YOU MUST CHOOSE!

Would you rather...

make a frittata with Philip Seymour Hoffman

OR

play Mastermind with Clint Eastwood?

Would you rather...

go to a strip club where all the strippers are crushes you had
in high school

OR

a strip club where all the strippers say what they are
actually thinking?

Would you rather...

once a day, feel the sensation of a good orgasm

OR

feel the feeling you got when you were a kid and you awoke to find it
snowing outside and that school was cancelled?

YOU MUST CHOOSE!

DATE, SCREW, KILL
Which of the three would you date, which would you screw, and which would you kill?

Heidi Montag, Taylor Swift, Aunt Jemima

Hulk Hogan, Donald Trump, Mario from video game fame

Jonah Hill, Michael Cera, Simon Cowell

Tin Man, Scarecrow, Cowardly Lion
Things to consider: giving your heart to the Tin Man, screwing your brains out with the Scarecrow, the Cowardly Lion = gay?

YOU MUST CHOOSE!

307

Would you rather...

be able to make anyone you touch have perfect 6 pack abs
OR
have an IQ of 140?

Would you rather never get...

tired **OR** hungry?

B.O. **OR** gas?

called "Dorkazon 2000" **OR** hit in the head with a pineapple?

Would you rather...

have sex with Zachary Quinto's Spock
OR
Leonard Nimoy's?

YOU MUST CHOOSE!

BACK THAT APP UP!

Would you rather...

have an app that tells you the size of a man's junk upon meeting him **OR** that translates what a guy is saying to what he is actually thinking?

an app that tells you how far a prospective date is willing to go **OR** that functions as birth control if you shine it on your privates for 30 seconds?

that works as a mirror **OR** as a throwing star?

YOU MUST CHOOSE!

Your most attractive friends invite you and your partner to have group sex. Would you rather participate or not?

Would you rather always be age...

5 **OR** 35?

12 **OR** 50?

2 **OR** 62?

YOU MUST CHOOSE!

Which would you rather use as an erotic food to enhance sex...

whipped cream **OR** melted chocolate?

A-1 sauce **OR** hard-boiled eggs?

Fun Dip **OR** gobstoppers?

Would you rather...

have sex with a "5"
OR
have sex with a "3" while a "10" watches?

YOU MUST CHOOSE!

Would you rather...

get a fifteen minute shopping spree (whatever you grab you keep)
in Dress Barn
OR
in a Macy's with a loose Siberian tiger?

Would you rather...

have an extra set of your gender's genitals anywhere you choose
on your body
OR
have the addition of the opposite gender's genitals on your body?
Things to consider: three-ways, one-ways, rainy days

YOU MUST CHOOSE!

Would you rather...

have your office's water cooler filled with malt liquor
OR
have Extremely Casual Friday (where everyone wears Daisy Duke shorts)?

Would you rather...

have access to live webcams of every room in the White House
OR
every room in your neighbors' houses?

YOU MUST CHOOSE!

Would you rather...

play video games for a job but make only minimum wage
OR
be a peep show booth cleaner and make $100,000 a year?

Would you rather...

live on the International Space Station for a month **OR**
on a tropical island?

live in a planetarium **OR** an amusement park?

on a tugboat **OR** in a ranch home with Dennis Eckersley?

Would you rather...

change the National Anthem to "Pants on the Ground"
(made famous on *American Idol*)
OR
change the words to the Pledge of Allegiance to the "Diarrhea Song"?
Things to consider: Place your hand over your heart and try both.

YOU MUST CHOOSE!

Would you rather...

watch your parents have a freestyle rap battle
OR
watch your parents have a freestyle dance battle?

Would you rather...

get to play "Truth or Dare" with famous celebrities
OR
famous historical figures?
Who would you choose to play with?
What would you ask them as a Truth?
What would dare them to do?

YOU MUST CHOOSE!

Would you rather...

have a kangaroo butler
OR
a monkey chauffeur?

Would you rather...

get ahead in life using your mind **OR** looks?

your connections **OR** your hard work?

your low post moves **OR** *Saved by The Bell* trivia knowledge?

Would you rather...

get to be a guest judge on *American Idol*
OR
get to force one of your friends to go on it?

YOU MUST CHOOSE!

Would you rather...

have a kitchen designed by the people that make
James Bond contraptions
OR
a bike designed by them?

Would you rather...

win a Grammy **OR** an Oscar?

a pro sport's MVP prize **OR** the Nobel Peace Prize?

a bocce tournament in front of a bunch of hot chicks **OR**
a Pro-Am charity golf tournament in front of no one?

YOU MUST CHOOSE!

Would you rather...

have your parents go on *Dancing with the Stars* **OR** *America's Got Talent?*

The Biggest Loser **OR** *What Not to Wear?*

The Apprentice **OR** *Top Chef?*

Would you rather...

get around by hovercraft
OR
pterodactyl?

Would you rather...

play Simon Says with Samuel L. Jackson
OR
go bowling with Michael Richards?

YOU MUST CHOOSE!

WORLD'S BEST VENEREAL DISEASES

Which of the following would you most want to have?

Genital diamonds

Sexually Transmitted MP3's

The Clap-on/Clap-off Clap

Vaginal ATM

Free Carpool Lane Gonorrhea

YOU MUST CHOOSE!

Which would you rather use as a sex toy...

a snuggie **OR** a menorah?

a wiffle ball **OR** a hand saw?

a cafeteria tray **OR** a credenza?

Would you rather...

have access to a Facebook for sex, where you can log in and see everyone your friends have had sex with, your friends' friends, the whole world interlocking in six degrees of separation
OR
not?

Would you rather...

play backgammon with Mandy Moore
OR
make popsicle crafts with Michelle Rodriguez?

YOU MUST CHOOSE!

Would you rather...

ride shotgun in a NASCAR race
OR
eliminate NASCAR from the planet?

Would you rather...

have a retractable ball-point pen in your finger
OR
have a laser pointer finger?

Would you rather...

have every part of your body be as pleasure-sensitive as your genitals
OR
not?

YOU MUST CHOOSE!

Would you rather live in a world where...

when dining at a restaurant, your laundry is done while you eat
OR
where all professional and doctor waiting rooms have a free,
full-time masseuse?

Would you rather live in a world where...

much like episodes of *Sesame Street*, the corporate sponsor of every
TV show is a letter/number
OR
where people vacation only by assuming the identities of others?

YOU MUST CHOOSE!

Would you rather live in a world where...

every person had a photographic memory

OR

x-ray vision?

Would you rather live in a world where...

animals had the same rights as people

OR

where animals had ketchup, mustard, and barbecue sauce in their blood?

YOU MUST CHOOSE!

CHAPTER SIXTEEN

WOULD YOU...?

"Everybody has a price… for the million dollar man."
—D.H. Lawrence

There's no such thing as a free lunch. Unless you feign interest in buying foods at Whole Foods where they are serving up free samples. That's it though: free samples at Whole Foods. Or I guess if you go to an art opening and eat all the cocktail food pretending to be interested in the art. But that's it: art openings and Whole Foods free samples. That's all. And wakes. You don't pay for wakes. Okay, so there are lots of free lunches. But not in this case. Here, there is a price to pay for whatever it is that you want.

Would you... get one DD breast implant for $900,000?

Would you... punch your grandmother in the stomach in order to get free cable for the rest of your life?

Would you... watch your parents have sex thrice to end world hunger?

Would you... Dutch-oven a 4-year-old orphan for an extra week's vacation at school/work?

Would you... sleep with the ugliest person at school/work (with no repercussions) for a promotion?

YOU MUST CHOOSE!

PANDA-MONIUM

Would you... mate with a panda if it meant saving 50 pandas every time you did it? How many times would you mate?

Would you... stop funding panda efforts and let nature take its course and have the panda go extinct?

Would you... hunt and kill 50 pandas with a bow and arrow to be able to have sex whenever and with whomever you choose?

YOU MUST CHOOSE!

Would you... lose an inch of height to gain two inches of length? (Women: "have your partner...")

Would you... berate an old woman for no reason for fifteen minutes in a closet with Jessica Alba? (Women: receive oral from Johnny Depp)?

Would you... drink forty bottles of ketchup in a row for $50,000?

YOU MUST CHOOSE!

Would you... remove your pants in public to establish a free WiFi hotspot?

Would you... sucker-punch your boss if there were absolutely no negative repercussions?

Would you... sleep your way up the ladder if you were attractive enough to pull it off? How about down the ladder if you're not?

Would you... love the one you're with if you can't be with the one you love?

YOU MUST CHOOSE!

Would you... have sex with Susan Boyle to have sex with Brooke Burke?

Would you... lick peanut butter off a dog's balls for your choice of season tickets to your favorite team or yearly Oscar tickets?

Would you... put on 70 pounds for a movie role? For $10,000? For the hell of it?

Would you... allow your wife or husband to make out with and feverishly grope a stranger one time in order to lower your mortgage interest rate by 1%?

YOU MUST CHOOSE!

Would you... screw Megan Fox/Brad Pitt if you knew a random person in the world would die because of it?

Would you... engage in heavy petting with Zac Efron in order to ensure there are no more *High School Musical* movies ever made again?

Would you... shoot seltzer water into the face of a homeless person in order to sleep with your choice of Taylor Lautner/ Alyssa Milano?

YOU MUST CHOOSE!

FOR THE LADIES

Would you... screw Hugh Jackman if it gave you shingles?

Would you... shave Alan Alda's balls for $500 a ball? Would you do both or just one?

Would you... date Mike Tyson for $1,000 a day? How many days would you last?

YOU MUST CHOOSE!

No one likes it when actors and actresses get mixed up in politics. Nonetheless, which of the following would you do?

Would you have sex with...

Hillary Clinton to get to have sex with your choice of Hilary Swank or Hilary Duff?

former Mexican President Vicente Fox to get to have sex with Megan Fox?

late Senator Strom Thurmond for Uma Thurman?

Jesse Jackson for Janet Jackson?

Michael Moore for your choice of Mandy or Demi Moore?

YOU MUST CHOOSE!

Would you... let Iron Chef Bobby Flay cook all your meals if it meant having to share a sleeping bag with him every night?

Would you... take an all-expense-paid vacation to Europe if you had to travel the whole time in a World War II motorcycle sidecar with Flavor Flav?

Would you... French kiss your pet for $100?

YOU MUST CHOOSE!

PUBLIC PRIVATES

Would you... slyly masturbate to completion on a public bus for $10,000?

at your office desk for $15,000?

in a Radio Shack from $18,000?

during a haircut for $35,000?

at a funeral for $50,000?

YOU MUST CHOOSE!

Would you... spend a month in space if it meant having to share the space station with the cast of *Jersey Shore*?

Would you... have one droopy eye if it meant being irresistibly attractive to librarians?

Would you... attend a stranger's wedding, vehemently claiming an ongoing relationship with the groom as well as the grandmother of the bride for $5000?

YOU MUST CHOOSE!

Would you... crash a funeral wearing fanatical sports fan attire (face paint, rainbow wig, posterboard using bold network letters in a contrived statement like "**E**ulogies **S**upport **P**allbearers' **N**otions," etc.) to stave off your own death for an extra two years?

Would you... perform a *Vagina Monologue*-esque rendition about your own genitalia to a packed theater for $10,000? How about a Diarrhea Monolouge where you recount your best stories of self-defecation?

Would you... legally change your name to Osama Bin Laden for $600,000 and a spelunking trip to Pakistan?

YOU MUST CHOOSE!

Would you... receive a pearl necklace from Louie Anderson if it turned into a real, high-quality pearl necklace? If this continued to happen, how many times would you engage?

Would you... administer reciprocal blumpkins with World Wrestling Entertainment's Mark Henry for $2 million?

Would you... spend a weekend having sex with Eva Mendes, if you had a 49% chance of catching genital warts?

Would you... dump your current friends to be best friends with (insert some celebrity?)

YOU MUST CHOOSE!

Would you... take half Bill Gates' fortune but have to be four times as nerdy?

Would you... get caught taking a dump on your neighbors' living room rug for free cell phone service?

Would you... eat a dog to save yours from being eaten?

Would you... live for a year in a fort you built when you were 9-years-old to live in your dream house for the following year?

YOU MUST CHOOSE!

Would you...

have sex with this guy

OR

this guy ?

YOU MUST CHOOSE!

SERIOUS QUESTIONS

Would you... give up sex for monk-like wisdom and calm of mind?

Would you... never have sex again for world peace?

Would you... punch a rabbi in the nose in order to get a BJ from Taylor Swift?

YOU MUST CHOOSE!

Would you... have a three way with Optimus Prime and Megatron to peacefully resolve the long-standing war between Decepticons and Autobots?

Would you... do Tyler Perry in drag for 1/100th of his wealth?

Would you... become a vegan for a year for a threesome with Natalie Portman and Zooey Deschanel?

Would you... miss a year of life with your partner in order to relive your senior year of college?

YOU MUST CHOOSE!

To have sex with your celebrity crush, would you...

consume a bottle of mayonnaise in ten minutes?

poop in your pants for a week?

carry a ladle around at all times in public for a year?

increase global temperature 1 degree immediately, drastically worsening global warming?

step on and squash a baby chick?

YOU MUST CHOOSE!

To have sex with your celebrity crush, would you...

eat 15 bull testicles?

not wear deodorant for a year?

get a genital piercing that has your keys attached to it?

change you legal name permanently to "Prelnar"?

sneak up behind you mom, and knock her legs out from under her?

YOU MUST CHOOSE!

Would you...

have sex with this woman

to have sex with this one?

YOU MUST CHOOSE!

CHAPTER SEVENTEEN

PRIVILEGES AND POSSESSIONS

Lucky you. The good times continue to roll. For reasons beyond your understanding, you are either being granted a prized possession (an object, creature, or person of great possibility) or a precious privilege (an honor, convenience, or enticing opportunity). What you do with your newfound blessing is up to you, as is the choice between two equally awesome options.

Would you rather...

have your face carved into Mt. Rushmore
OR
have your ass carved into Mt. Rushmore?

Who would you rather have in your camp at Burning Man?

ventriloquist Jeff Dunham **OR** Al Roker?

Johnny Depp from *Pirates of the Caribbean* **OR** Johnny Depp from *Alice in Wonderland?*

Socrates **OR** Fozzie Bear?

Marilyn Manson and Charles Manson **OR** the Dalai Lama and Dolly Parton?

YOU MUST CHOOSE!

Would you rather...

have a Real Sex Doll in the likeness of Jenna Haze **OR** Wonder Woman?

an anonymous hot woman **OR** the celebrity of your choice?

Harriet Tubman **OR** a hot Klingon woman?

Would you rather...

have a huge table-top iPad (â la table-top Pac Man at Pizza Hut)
OR
a Bluetooth head?

YOU MUST CHOOSE!

CREATURE FEATURES

Would you rather...

have a highly trained ferret that handles your postage and DVD return
OR
a highly trained chinchilla that lathers up and luffas you in the shower each morning?

Would you rather...

have a genetically engineered caterpillar that crawls to wherever you have an itch and scratches it
OR
a genetically created tiny hummingbird that cleans your nostrils, ears, belly button, and in between your toes?

YOU MUST CHOOSE!

Would you rather...

have a really smart bomb-sniffing dog who can locate anyone who would be attracted to you

OR

have a magical inch worm who can locate any g-spot?

Would you rather...

have a voodoo mouse that allowed you to drag and drop people in real life as if they were on a computer screen

OR

have a photo-editing program that actually made people change to whatever you did to them on screen?

Things to consider: How would you use your drag and drop powers? Would you use them for good or evil? What photo-editing would you do? Who would you use it on?

YOU MUST CHOOSE!

GETTING CARDED

Would you rather...

have a "Get out of trouble at work" card (no matter what you do, one time, you won't get in trouble)

OR

have a "Get out of trouble at home" card (same rules)?

Would you rather...

have a "Get out of jail free" card (no matter what you do, one time you will not go to jail)

OR

a "get a free Starbucks coffee a day for life" card?

Would you rather...

have a set of fake ID's that each actually create the life that they identify you as while in your wallet

OR

yellow and red cards you can give out at work (like a soccer ref) to get someone warned and fired?

YOU MUST CHOOSE!

Would you rather...

have the ability to know the answer to any trivia question, but only as long as you're completely naked

OR

have the ability to be invisible but only when spastically dancing?

Would you rather...

be able to go days without water but have a camel-like hump on your back

OR

have the saying "you are what you eat" become reality, though only affecting your hands?

Would you rather...

have a hat that styles your hair when you put it on

OR

have shoes that massage your feet with the flick of a switch?

YOU MUST CHOOSE!

Would you rather...

have seven samurai sworn to protect you **OR** seven ninjas?

5 dragons **OR** 2 wizards?

4000 hamsters **OR** 10 guidance counselors?

Would you rather...

have a pill that instantly makes you sober
OR
be able to teleport home after a night of heavy drinking no matter where you are?

Would you rather...

be permitted to backhand-slap a far-too-chipper coworker on a particularly painful Monday morning with no repercussions
OR
give your boss the finger with no repercussions?

YOU MUST CHOOSE!

Would you rather...

have one use of a morning after pill

OR

one use of a 10-years-after pill?

Would you rather...

never have to wait for an elevator

OR

always jump to the front of the list in karaoke?

YOU MUST CHOOSE!

Would you rather...

have a magic pair of glasses that allows you see what Ted Danson is seeing

OR

have magic earphones that allow you to hear what George Washington Carver's girlfriend was hearing back in time?

Would you rather...

have self-flossing teeth

OR

have an anus that manicures nails?

Would you rather...

have any member of the opposite sex's thoughts text messaged to you at any time

OR

be able to control any member of the opposite sex for up to an hour using a Sony Playstation video game controller?

YOU MUST CHOOSE!

Who would you rather have in your bedroom during sex?

a wise grizzled golf caddy who stands by the side of the bed and offers you tips on your form during sex

OR

a tennis ball boy who quickly sprints across the bed puts it back in anytime it slips out?

Who would you rather have in your bedroom during sex?

the ghost of Ed McMahon to cheer for and corroborate you ("Yesss!")

OR

a Jet Blue steward who thanks your guest for choosing you and offers them a complimentary beverage?

YOU MUST CHOOSE!

Would you rather live in a world where...

all war criminals are successfully tried and convicted

OR

where everyone who says words like "over-exaggerate" and "irregardless" without recognizing the linguistic redundancy is successfully tried and convicted?

Would you rather...

have a fountain of couth

OR

a Midas touch (everything you touch turns to a muffler)?

YOU MUST CHOOSE!

Would you rather...

have charade sex

OR

have UPS chart sex where you draw doodles that become dirty by erasing or adding lines?

Would you rather...

be fluent in Latin

OR

Pig-Latin?

YOU MUST CHOOSE!

Bird-buffs only
Would you rather...

watch a pilated woodpecker excavate a nest
OR
a bluebird feed mealworms to its brood?

Would you rather...

have a loyal entourage of game show hosts
OR
janitors?

Would you rather...

have a 50-inch ADHD TV which can't stay on any channel for more
than ten seconds at a time
OR
have a big, clunky, old, rotary phone as your cell phone?

YOU MUST CHOOSE!

Would you rather...

get $1,000 anytime you punch a random person in their face
OR
get $10,000 anytime you get punched in the face?

Which of the following would you rather be able to indulge in consequence-free...

cigarettes **OR** promiscuity?

indulgent foods **OR** hard drugs?

telling crying kids in public to shut up **OR** crying and demanding a juice box whenever you don't get your way?

YOU MUST CHOOSE!

Would you rather...

be able to commune with birds to direct them exactly where to take a doo-doo

OR

have ear speakers that broadcast whatever music or sound you imagine in your head

Would you rather...

be able to speak with dead people, but only the perverts

OR

be able to read the minds of people named Ludwig?

Would you rather...

make anyone you want have a beer gut

OR

be able to literally shed pounds?

YOU MUST CHOOSE!

Would you rather...

play Wii basketball vs. Kobe Bryant
OR
that vibrating football game vs. Peyton Manning?

Would you rather...

have the ability to send unlimited text messages to yourself
five minutes ago
OR
be able to sell a lame Jim Carrey movie based on the premise
for $5,000,000?

YOU MUST CHOOSE!

CHAPTER EIGHTEEN

DEATHS, INCONVENIENCES, AND OTHER THINGS THAT SUCK

To paraphrase Benjamin Franklin, "There are only two certainties in life: death and annoying shit." And sometimes the latter makes you wish for the former. How we bear struggle and suffering is the true test of our character. It's time to find out what you are truly made of.

Would you rather...

get Indian-burned to death
OR
noogied to death?

Would you rather...

have the Russian government determine the weather
OR
a cabal of 13-year-old girls determine your Netflix queue?

Would you rather...

have your child be raised by hyenas
OR
by pageant mothers?

YOU MUST CHOOSE!

Who would you rather have as an arch enemy?

an anteater **OR** juggler?

Bill Cosby **OR** Bill Nye (the Science Guy)

a vengeful CPA **OR** a cock-blocking warlock?

Would you rather...

commute every day through a paparazzi-infested red carpet
OR
via parade?

YOU MUST CHOOSE!

Would you rather...

be sautéed to death

OR

catapulted to your death?

Would you rather hell be...

trying to straighten impossible-to-straighten Venetian blinds

OR

a never-ending airport security line?

YOU MUST CHOOSE!

Would you rather...

have to talk like a robot for a whole day
OR
walk like a robot for a whole day?
Try doing each all day.

Would you rather...

have to walk with your feet never leaving the ground
OR
never be able to use the same word twice in any given 24-hour period?
Try each for a day.

Would you rather...

survive by eating lima beans and mustard for a week
OR
Brussels sprouts and prune juice?
Make a deal with your friend, designating one food
you can eat. See who can go longer.

YOU MUST CHOOSE!

Would you rather...

have as a conjoined twin, a constantly fussy baby
OR
a 1987 Ford Escort?

Would you rather...

have to drive twice the speed limit
OR
half the speed limit?

Would you rather...

be able to drink only by shotgunning cans
OR
bathe using only a turkey baster and water?

YOU MUST CHOOSE!

Would you rather...

have to brew your daily cup of coffee by peeing into the coffee maker
OR
never be able to flush your toilet?

Would you rather...

be able to only date friends of your mother's
OR
convicts with two strikes?

Would you rather...

get bedazzled to death
OR
drown in a bowl of Apple Jacks?

YOU MUST CHOOSE!

Would you rather...

emphatically boo anytime you see a postman

OR

after watching every business presentation, break out in a sarcastic slow clap and say "Well, well, well... looks like the student has become the teacher."

Would you rather...

have to wade through a dumpster full of garbage until you found a contact lens each morning

OR

have to retrieve a penny as quickly as possible in a shallow pool full of piranha?

YOU MUST CHOOSE!

Would you rather...

get literal Athlete's Foot (have one foot mutate into the foot of your favorite athelete)

OR

get literal Shingles on your back?

Would you rather...

have to wear three layers of sweats whenever you go to the beach

OR

have to wear your mom's bathing suit?

Would you rather...

drown in vomit

OR

blood?

YOU MUST CHOOSE!

Would you rather...

never again cut your finger nails
OR
never cut your hair?

Would you rather...

appear in all photos in black and white
OR
appear in all refections as Nick Nolte?

YOU MUST CHOOSE!

Would you rather...

get stuck on an elevator with gossipy girls **OR** Eastern European businessmen talking loudly on their cell phones?

skunks **OR** angry sumo wrestlers?

100 hornets **OR** (insert annoying person you know)?

Would you rather...

lay an egg and have to sit on it like a bird
OR
have to hibernate like a bear each winter from November to March?

YOU MUST CHOOSE!

Would you rather have sex with the hybrid...

LeBron James Gandolfini **OR** Jason Alexander Ovechkin?

Larry David Beckham **OR** Danica Patrick Stewart?

Lawrence Taylor Swift **OR** Carly Simon Cowell?

Kim Kardashian McKellen **OR** Rosie Perez Hilton?

Della Reese Witherspoon **OR** Sonia Sotomayor McCheese?

Things to consider: Same thing, but who would you rather have sex with?

YOU MUST CHOOSE!

Would you rather...

be caught by aliens and placed in an alien zoo
OR
be used for alien scientific research?

Would you rather...

have Vulcan ears
OR
a Vulcan personality?

Would you rather...

hear all voices as the voice of Larry King
OR
see all people as animated *Simpsons* characters?

YOU MUST CHOOSE!

Would you rather...

be allergic to all members of the opposite sex that are an "8"
or more attractive

OR

be severely allergic to all members of the opposite sex under an "8"?

Would you rather...

be unable to distinguish between sandwiches and man-eating tigers

OR

between your pet and a head of lettuce?

Would you rather...

wake up with a different stranger every morning

OR

wake up looking like a different stranger every morning?

YOU MUST CHOOSE!

Would you rather...

be the minister of tourism for Zimbabwe
OR
camp director at a camp of little, snotty, fat kids?

Would you rather...

mistake a tube of super glue for toothpaste
OR
lubricant?

YOU MUST CHOOSE!

Would you rather...

have to air your "singing in the car moments" on YouTube

OR

have to explain the terms in this book—such as "arabian goggles" and "cleveland steamer"—to your parents?

Would you rather...

get stung by a thousand wasps

OR

have to listen to El DeBarge's "In the Rhythm of the Night" 1000 times in a week?

Would you rather...

be followed by a personal heckler

OR

have a cricket that follows you around, chirping after your jokes and during all awkward silences in your conversations?

YOU MUST CHOOSE!

Would you rather...

every time you're in a car, have to hang your head out the window like a dog

OR

have to sleep curled up at the end of your parents' bed like a dog?

Would you rather...

for the rest of your life, only be able to make right turns

OR

left turns?

Would you rather...

have to hitchhike with strangers to get anywhere

OR

have to wear/use diapers and depend on strangers to change them?

YOU MUST CHOOSE!

Would you rather have to earn a living using only...

a kazoo **OR** chalk?

a dreidel **OR** six lemons?

a spatula and a jar of pearl onions **OR** your hair and a crinkled photo of Joy Behar?

Would you rather...

drink a cup of hot bacon grease
OR
of someone else's spit?

YOU MUST CHOOSE!

Would you rather...

hunt
OR
gather?

Would you rather spend a year deprived of...

water **OR** coffee?

wine **OR** dessert?

pants **OR** vowels?

YOU MUST CHOOSE!

Would you rather...

your refrigerator automatically charge your credit card with mini-bar prices
OR
have all of your Internet-viewed pornography appear on your credit card statement at a dollar a minute?

Would you rather...

swap net worth and wardrobes with Steve Jobs
OR
Bill Gates?

Would you rather...

dress exclusively in merchandise from PetSmart
OR
eat food exclusively from PetSmart?

YOU MUST CHOOSE!

CHAPTER NINETEEN

FUN QUESTIONS FOR YOUR CHURCH YOUTH GROUP

Hey all! Here are some delightfully fun questions to get your church youth group talking. They're certain to make you think. And you just might spark a chuckle too.

Would you rather...

have to wear a scarf that your grandma knit from her pubic hair every day for a winter

OR

get hair plugs from your own pubic hair?

Would you rather...

die via bullet to head

OR

slow asphyxiation by a hairy 1970s vagina?

YOU MUST CHOOSE!

Would you rather...

lick Mo'Nique's asscrack
OR
a mound of bat guano?

Would you rather...

be caught masturbating to pictures of your ex
OR
the Hamburglar?

Would you rather...

get "dog-in-a-bath-tub'd" by Brian Williams
OR
receive an enema from Carrot Top?
Things to consider: Google it.

YOU MUST CHOOSE!

Would you rather...

be the biggest person at a little person orgy

OR

the youngest person at a nursing home orgy?

Would you rather...

have a tractor beam anus

OR

a hover vagina?

YOU MUST CHOOSE!

Would you rather wipe your ass with...

poison ivy **OR** dry ice?

a split habanero pepper **OR** your bare hand?

a steel wool pad **OR** your cat?

Would you rather...

get leg-humped by ten *Twilight* werewolves
OR
get "hot Karl'd" by the creatures in *Where the Wild Things Are?*
Things to consider: Google it.

YOU MUST CHOOSE!

Which would you rather have happen to Osama Bin Laden?

have a glass beaker shoved up his urethra and then shattered
OR
have him discover he has been eating pulled pork sandwiches for a year without realizing it?

Would you rather...

blindside tackle your grandma
OR
give her ten seconds of mouth to mouth?

YOU MUST CHOOSE!

Would you rather...

suck on your high school English teacher's nipples
OR
frog intestines?

Would you rather...

find a sex video of your best friend and your boyfriend/girlfriend
OR
of your parents?

YOU MUST CHOOSE!

Would you rather...

watch a stripper who was 80-years-old **OR** 400 pounds?

who keeps farting audibly and potently **OR** who looks a little like your mom?

who dances '80s breakdancing **OR** does a Stomp routine?

Would you rather...

play strip poker with the cast of *The View*
OR
60 Minutes?

YOU MUST CHOOSE!

Would you rather...

delicately place your penis in the mouth of a cow
OR
in a French fry fryer?

Would you rather...

receive a Cleveland Steamer from your partner
OR
a $5,000 parking ticket?

YOU MUST CHOOSE!

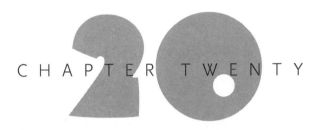

CHAPTER TWENTY

WHO'D YOU RATHER...?
PART 2:
ELECTRIC BOOGALOO

Still looking for that perfect somebody? The yin to your sexual yang? Well, your yang need not be alone much longer. Luckily there are plenty more people, robots, mascots, cartoons, and inanimate objects to sift through. So keep plugging away until you find Mr. or Mrs. Right (or at least Mr. or Mrs. Right Angle!) Wait, no... that's not how it goes.

Would you rather...

have sex with Sam Worthington's paraplegic marine character in *Avatar* **OR** his blue alien avatar?

Prince Henry **OR** Prince William?

Mr. Rogers **OR** Captain Kangaroo?

YOU MUST CHOOSE!

Would you rather have sex with...

any four cast members from the show *Glee*, then have them do a musical number about it **OR** any four cast members of *Saturday Night Live*, then have them perform a comedy sketch about it?

have sex with your choice of Reese Witherspoon/Jason Bateman and have everybody know about it **OR** have sex with your choice of Megan Fox/Johnny Depp and have no one know about it?

YOU MUST CHOOSE!

(IM)PERFECT PARTNERS

Would you rather...

have a sex partner who always ejaculates prematurely after one minute **OR** one who ejaculates 2 days postmaturely wherever they are?

have sex with Penelope Cruz if she spoke dirty in a Spanish accent **OR** Heidi Klum if she spoke dirty in a frightening German accent?

Barry Manilow if he then wrote you a love song **OR** Eminem if he then wrote a hateful rap about you?

have sex with Salma Hayek's body but with your face on it **OR** with your body with Salma Hayek's face (genitals remain female)?

YOU MUST CHOOSE!

Would you rather...

be attacked by ninjas while having sex with a supermodel
OR
vice-versa?

Would you rather...

have cowgirl sex with a missionary
OR
missionary sex with a cowgirl?
Things to consider: conversion, spurs

YOU MUST CHOOSE!

Would you rather watch a discovered sex tape with...

Brad Pitt and Angelina Jolie **OR** Barack and Michelle Obama?

Yao Ming and Christina Ricci **OR** Tracy Morgan and Vanessa Hudgens?

the contestants on the last *Biggest Loser* (pre-weight loss) in an orgy **OR** your parents?

a camel and a koala bear **OR** two deaf people?

Johnny Depp and Julia Child **OR** the Gumbel brothers and Eliza Dushku?

Would you rather...

screw a janitor on a space ship
OR
an astronaut in a janitor's closet?

YOU MUST CHOOSE!

Which threesome partners would you rather have?

former couple Padma Lakshmi and Salman Rushdie **OR** Woody Allen and Soon Yi?

Jerry Lewis and Juliette Lewis **OR** Tom Brady and Mrs. Brady?

Sienna Miller and Dennis Miller **OR** Halle Berry and Frankenberry?

YOU MUST CHOOSE!

Would you rather...

have sex with this guy

OR

this guy?

YOU MUST CHOOSE!

Would you rather...

have sex with Abe Lincoln

OR

George Washington?

Would you rather...

have sex with Ashley Olsen if she lost 50 pounds

OR

Kirstie Alley if she gained 50 pounds?

Would you rather...

have sex with someone who you are able to apply Photoshop effects to in real life

OR

someone who could do an impression of anyone perfectly?

Things to consider: Dragon wings would look awesome!; possible impressions: porn stars, movie stars, Don Rickles, your old girlfriend/boyfriend

YOU MUST CHOOSE!

Would you rather...

play spin the bottle with the cast of *Baywatch* **OR** the cast of *Gilligan's Island?*

the cast of the new *90210* **OR** the old *90210?*

with the crew of *Star Trek: The Next Generation* **OR** *Star Trek: Voyager?*

Things to consider: Vulcans possess nearly three times the strength of humans, *Voyager's* Holodeck has slightly more advanced graphics than *Enterprise's*, 7 of 9's nature is to comply with the will of the collective, Counselor Troy is only half Betazoid ... y'know, if you're into that sort of thing.

YOU MUST CHOOSE!

MASH-UPS!

Which of the following hybrids would you rather have sex with?

Kirk Cameron Diaz **OR** Tera Patrick Dempsey?

Rachael Ray Lewis **OR** Liv Tyler Perry?

Robert Blake Lively **OR** Nate Hayden Panettiere?

YOU MUST CHOOSE!

405

Would you rather...

have sex with everyone who has ever held a Guinness World Record for a physical oddity or deformity

OR

all of the people who have ever appeared as a guest on the *Jerry Springer Show?*

Things to consider: fat twins on motorcycles, long nails dude, World's most rotund knees guy

Would you rather...

have sex with a half-sized J-Lo

OR

a double-sized J-Lo?

Would you rather...

have sex with Jessica Biel but get crabs

OR

make out with Meredith Vieira and get a free Big Gulp?

YOU MUST CHOOSE!

Would you rather...

have sex with the Quaker Oats mascot in a bed of his oatmeal

OR

Uncle Ben in a bed of his rice?

Things to consider: Both will be done in under 5 minutes.

Would you rather...

have sex with Emeril Lagasse and then have him cook a four-course meal for you

OR

Christian Bale and then have him chew you out for not getting something right?

YOU MUST CHOOSE!

Would you rather have sex with...

this woman

OR

this woman?

YOU MUST CHOOSE!

Would you rather...

have sex with Grace Park **OR** Mila Kunis?

Jenna Jameson **OR** Tila Tequila?

Elizabeth Berkley **OR** Elisabeth Hasselbeck?

Tiffani-Amber Thiessen **OR** Tiffani Thiessen?

Would you rather...

have an orgy with an NFL team after they've just won the Super Bowl
OR
after they've just lost the Super Bowl?

YOU MUST CHOOSE!

Would you rather...

have sex with Kristen Stewart from *Twilight* **OR** Anna Paquin from *True Blood*?

with Jorja Fox on the set of *CSI* **OR** one of the models on the set of the *Price is Right*?

with a woman with no hair **OR** a woman with a soul patch?

the cast of *Jersey Shore* **OR** the creatures in Jabba the Hutt's fortress?

Would you rather...

have sex with Johnny Depp with facial hair **OR** clean-shaven Johnny Depp?

Alan Greenspan with a 12-inch schlong **OR** Derek Jeter with a one-incher?

Keith Richards **OR** an Oompa-Loompa?

YOU MUST CHOOSE!

Would you rather...

have sex with John Madden
OR
assume his physique?

Would you rather...

have sex with Gary Busey
OR
have his brain for a month?

Would you rather...

have humiliating submissive sex with Janet Reno
OR
have armpit sex with Aretha Franklin?

YOU MUST CHOOSE!

Would you rather...

have sex with a Russian female shot-putter
OR
an exotic evil Russian spy who may or may not try to kill you?

Would you rather...

see Bill Clinton naked
OR
Hillary?

YOU MUST CHOOSE!

Would you rather...

have phone sex with Rosie Perez **OR** Paula Abdul?

Celine Dion in French **OR** Jenna Jameson in Yiddish?

Terry Bradshaw **OR** Shannon Sharpe?

Penn **OR** Teller?

Russell Crowe **OR** the Rock?

Matt Lauer **OR** Tom Cruise but he's on speaker phone and there's like a lot of background noise and stuff and he's like clearly checking emails at the same time?

YOU MUST CHOOSE!

Would you rather...

be more sympathetic toward someone who goes to rehab for racism (Mel Gibson)
OR
sex (Tiger Woods)?

Would you rather...

be forced to listen to Joan Rivers assess all of your sexual encounters
OR
be forced to listen to Howard Stern assess all of your sexual encounters?

Would you rather...

have sex with Barack Obama
OR
Mitt Romney?

YOU MUST CHOOSE!

Would you rather...

spend one weekend a month as Snoop Dogg's girlfriend
OR
as Snoop Dogg's lawyer?

Would you rather...

have sex with a being with the face of Zach Efron but the body/ wardrobe of Larry the Cable Guy
OR
a being with the body of Brad Pitt and the face of George Washington?

YOU MUST CHOOSE!

Check out these other *Would You Rather...?* titles, available at bookstores and online retailers.

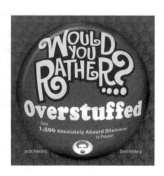  

www.sevenfooterpress.com